ISLAND
EATS

Signature Chefs'
Recipes from
Vancouver Island
and the Salish Sea

ISLAND

DAWN POSTNIKOFF

JOANNE SASVARI

PORT HARDY

CAMPBELL
RIVER

COMOX
COURTENAY

HORNBY
ISLAND

QUALICUM BEACH

PARKSVILLE

TOFINO

PORT
ALBERNI

UCLUELET

NANAIMO

LADYSMITH

GALIANO
ISLAND

DUNCAN

SALT SPRING
ISLAND

MILL BAY

SOUTH PENDER
ISLAND

BRENTWOOD
BAY

VICTORIA

EATS

Figure.1

Vancouver / Berkeley

Dedicated to all of you who keep all of us so very well-fed.
Thank you.

Recipes are chef tested

21 22 23 24 25 5 4 3 2 1

Cataloguing data is available from Library and Archives Canada
ISBN 978-1-77327-167-5 (hbk.)

Design by Naomi MacDougall
Food photography by Gabriel Cabrera
Portrait and ancillary photography by Danika McDowell
except pages 50 and 76
Food styling by Bri Beaudoin
Food styling assisting by Sophie MacKenzie
Prop styling by Naomi MacDougall
Cover and interior illustrations by Ben Frey

Editing by Michelle Meade
Copy editing by Pam Robertson
Proofreading by Merel Elsinga
Indexing by Iva Cheung

Printed and bound in China by C&C Offset Printing Co.
Distributed internationally by Publishers Group West

Figure 1 Publishing Inc.
Vancouver BC Canada
www.figure1publishing.com

Figure 1 Publishing works in the traditional, unceded territory of the Xʷməθkʷəy̓əm (Musqueam), Sḵwx̱wú7mesh (Squamish) and Səl̓ílwətaʔɬ (Tsleil-Waututh) peoples.

Recipe Notes

Unless stated otherwise:

Butter is unsalted.

Citrus juices are freshly squeezed.

Eggs are large.

Flour is all-purpose.

Herbs are fresh.

Milk is whole.

Pepper is black and freshly ground.

Produce is medium-sized.

Salt is kosher (not coarse).

Sugar is granulated.

CONTENTS

FOREWORD

In the late seventies, my brilliant, creative, hardworking wife Frédérique and I opened the Sooke Harbour House, one of North America's first restaurants to be recognized for its farm-to-table localist model, a pioneer in the use of edible flowers, seaweeds, First Nations' foods and wild indigenous ingredients such as mushrooms and berries.

We were very fortunate to receive recognition for it, too. Sooke Harbour House was named the "Best Restaurant in the World for Authentic, Local Cuisine" by *Gourmet* magazine and the *Globe and Mail*'s Joanne Kates called it the "Best Restaurant in Canada." Frédérique and I were both recipients of the Governor General of Canada's Nation's Table Award for Inspiration and Mentorship, Canada's top food-related award.

So, why am I forewording this book? I know, better than most, how the islands' culinary culture has evolved in the last forty years. And if pleasurable dining or culinary tourism is your focus, this book will provide you with a delicious introduction to the foods and restaurants of our region and insights into the worthy people behind them.

In short, *Island Eats* is a good guide to one of the world's most promising emerging culinary regions: Vancouver Island and the Canadian Gulf Islands.

In a globalizing world, more diners are seeking a sense of place, the flavour of locality. This cookbook gives us a chance to connect with island food and familiarize ourselves with the stewards of our land and sea. Thanks to the hard work of many chefs, artisans and suppliers over the past forty years, the islands region is increasingly gaining recognition as a destination on the international culinary tourist map. This book will lead you to the doorstep of several culinary treasures.

On the islands, we are quite different from Vancouver and other cities. To a much greater degree, we buy from local farms or grow our own produce. Many of us have direct relationships with farmers, foragers, fishermen and suppliers. We tend to be more seasonal and, wherever possible, use ingredients that are ethical, organic, free range and natural. Our restaurants are often smaller, cosier and more relaxed.

Many of the chefs in this book are guided by shared values and espouse some level of localism. They embrace the return to localized food production, transformation and consumption, based on very direct relationships between restaurants, consumers, farmers, foragers and fishermen. They work with local farmers and play a major role in protecting against biodiversity loss through their purchasing power and influence with the public. At a time when more than half the world's calories come from a few species of rice, corn and wheat, a time when less and less seed is available for fewer and fewer choices of foods, regional chefs who support local farms buy a wide variety of ingredients that support greater food biodiversity.

Localism is not really about a "100-mile diet," which would take us far out of the islands' bio-region. The localism I am referring to embraces all elements of the exchanges in our food community. Localism is about direct relationships and trust amongst all those who provide the ingredients and cook the meals that we eat within a somewhat sustainable food system.

It's good for your health, too. Most foods develop many of their nutritional qualities in the last week of ripening. If you are buying your food locally and seasonally, at the peak of its ripeness, you will be eating much healthier food than if it is shipped unripe from California, Mexico or China. And food tastes much better when you use the right local ingredients, in season.

Forty-plus years ago, when we started Sooke Harbour House, barely anyone beyond the Salish Sea paid attention to islands food. Since then, countless chefs, producers, restaurant owners, Indigenous leaders and academics have played an immeasurable role in the evolution of our regional cuisine.

Among those who pioneered the kind of regional food featured in this book was scholar, food writer and champion of Canadian cuisine Anita Stewart, who sadly died in late 2020. She played a prodigious, inspirational part in fostering our islands cuisine, and promoting it right across the country.

Our friend, the ethnobotanist Dr. Nancy Turner, has contributed enormously to our understanding of wild foods and the First Nations' 14,000-plus years of food knowledge. Chefs and home cooks alike are discovering this historic connection thanks to the teachings of people like Dolly and Anna Watts of the Gitk'san First Nation, John Bradley Williams of the Tsawout Nation and Heiltsuk Hereditary Chief Harvey Humchitt and his wife, Brenda. We are all better for learning from their philosophy of living in harmony with the land.

Many chefs have led the evolution of islands cooking over the last four decades. Among them: Mara Jernigan, formerly of Fairburn Farm, who played a major role in putting the Cowichan Valley on the international culinary map; Lisa Ahier, chef-owner of SoBo, who did the same for Tofino; and Bill Jones, owner of Deerholme Farm, who has taught countless people about islands food through his cookbooks and cooking classes. Others include: Andrea Carlson, Melissa Craig, Edward Tuson, James Walt and Peter Zambri.

Thanks to all of these people, and so many others, the islands now have a reputation for good food. Culinary surprises are hidden away in some of the remotest island recesses and more culinary tourists are drawn to the islands than ever before.

Use this book to help map out your trip.

My own culinary adventures will involve visiting the Swept Away Inn at the dock in Port Alberni and going out mushrooming with Daniel and Bouchra Savard to see what Moroccan food that "relies heavily on organic ingredients from local farms" tastes like.

I can't wait. After all, what could be better in life than a bottle of wine or a craft beer, the food from these islands, and the good conversation that goes with them?

SINCLAIR PHILIP

INTRODUCTION

Plenty of people talk about farm-to-table dining these days. But on Vancouver Island and the Gulf Islands of the Salish Sea, it's truly a way of life. And why not, when there is so much abundance to choose from? From Port Hardy to the Saanich Peninsula, the rain-soaked west coast to the sun-drenched Gulf Islands, farmers grow everything from truffles to tea, passionfruit to Pinot Noir, water buffalo to the most delicately briny oysters.

Beyond the farms, there are the wild foods of the forests and ocean. Sockeye salmon. Dungeness crab. Spot prawns. Halibut. Wild mushrooms. Blackberries, salmon berries, huckleberries. The mysterious cynamoka berry. The scandalous-looking giant clam called the geoduck.

Is it any wonder then that so many talented chefs are finding their way here? In the following pages, we will introduce you to some of the islands' best, their signature dishes and the passionate culinary community they've built here on the edge of the continent.

Created by volcanic activity some 150 million years ago, Vancouver Island is a long, narrow wedge of land along Canada's west coast. It's 460 kilometres long and 100 kilometres at its widest point, with a rugged mountain range snaking down its spine. The island's darkly forested west coast faces the Pacific Ocean and all the rainstorms it can hurl at it. Its rain-shadowed east coast is a place of

fertile farmland and fast-growing communities like Nanaimo, Parksville and Comox. Between the island and the mainland, the pretty Gulf Islands dot the Salish Sea, their protected harbours luring boaters and artists alike. And at the island's southern tip is Victoria, the provincial capital, known for its afternoon teas, cosy pubs and a dynamic young food scene fed by three surrounding agricultural regions.

For millennia, these lands and waters have been home to the Indigenous Coast Salish, Kwakw<u>aka</u>'wakw and Nuu-chah-nulth peoples whose culture is still such a quintessential part of life here. Europeans first arrived in the eighteenth century, seeking fish, furs, timber and fame. In 1778, Captain James Cook sailed into Nootka Sound, took one look and knew a good thing when he saw it—he promptly claimed the place for Britain, and there is still a certain English influence here, from the groomed flower gardens and ye olde Tudorbethan architecture to the ubiquitous fish 'n' chips.

Since then, of course, many other people have arrived, some to visit for a short while, others to stay for a lifetime. But this is not a place people tend to stumble upon. It's not on the way to somewhere else. Everyone who is here has chosen to be here. Often, they are the seekers, searching for peace or adventure, beauty or fortune: the hippies, poets and artists, as well as the loggers, fishers and farmers who carve a living from the land and the sea. They all find a home here.

And these days, so do the chefs, and the people hungry for what they are cooking.

Not all that long ago, dining out on Vancouver Island meant a bowl of chowder in some cosy pub, or maybe a steak, if you wanted to be really fancy. The best food was served at home. Salmon grilled over a cedar fire on the beach. Dungeness crab boiled in a pot of seawater and served with sweet drawn butter. Pie filled with tart blackberries plucked from the brambles in the backyard. Tender oysters shucked and slurped right on the dock.

Then in 1979, Frédérique and Sinclair Philip purchased Sooke Harbour House, a white clapboard inn with a small dining room and a rambling garden, perched on a rocky spit about forty-five minutes west of Victoria. He went diving for uni (sea urchin) and sea asparagus; she grew edible flowers and heirloom vegetables when no one had heard of such a thing. Guests arrived from all over the world, hungry for the kind of hyper-local food the Philips were serving. Sooke Harbour House quickly gained a reputation as "Chez Panisse North," and became an inspiration for chefs, producers and farmers alike.

Sadly, Sooke Harbour House was sold in 2020, its future uncertain. But its legacy lives on at Victoria's 10 Acres Bistro (page 16), which has its own farm, and at Pluvio Restaurant + Rooms (page 130) in Ucluelet, where edible flowers grow on the roof, and at Oxeye (page 120) on Galiano Island, a casual café whose three rising-star chefs forage for the kind of ingredients big-city chefs pay a fortune for, if they can get their hands on them at all.

In the last twenty years, dozens and dozens of talented chefs have moved to Vancouver Island and the Gulf Islands. Even in the smallest communities, you'll find chefs who've worked and staged in Michelin-starred restaurants or owned their own storied establishments elsewhere. They're shucking oysters and rolling pasta just for you, pouring you a glass of local wine, or telling you about the best surf beach or hiking trail or the cool new craft brewery in town. They're just happy to live and cook in a place where the air is clean, the ingredients are unparalleled and the people are open-minded and open-hearted.

In these pages they share some of their favourite recipes, the kind of soul-satisfying dishes you will want to make again and again. They are ones they make themselves—not just for their customers, but for their families— from ingredients grown by their friends and neighbours.

And if all of this makes Vancouver Island and the Gulf Islands sound just a little too magical, just that tiny bit too good to be true, well, you'll just have to come and taste for yourself. Who knows? You might not leave either.

THE RESTAURANTS

THE RECIPES

Starters and Little Meals

Brunch Fare

Salads, Soups and Sides

(V) = Vegetarian

10 ACRES BISTRO

Marcelo Najarro

Mike Murphy's North Saanich farm is, to be precise, 10.014 acres. There, he grows fruit, vegetables and herbs, raises turkeys, ducks and pigs (which are fed with the kitchen scraps from the restaurant) and hosts the occasional long-table dinner. "I bought the farm in a fit of pique when the city announced that we had to separate our compost," the long-time Victoria restaurateur admits with a laugh. "The learning curve was steep."

Murphy was born and raised in Victoria and for years had owned and operated several iconic Victoria restaurants, including Cecconi's Trattoria, Il Terrazzo, Bon Rouge Bistro (which later became 10 Acres Bistro) and Pescatores Fish House and Oyster Bar (now known as the Commons), which was housed in a heritage building just steps from the Inner Harbour. But then he read an article about farming out east and realized, "The Saanich Peninsula has outstanding farmland and better growing conditions." He bought the farm to feed his restaurant kitchen, then loved the name so much he renamed Bon Rouge after it.

The concept is casual upscale, locally sourced, authentic comfort food, from a kitchen led by executive chef Marcelo Najarro. "We do it the old-fashioned way," Murphy says. "We make our own stocks and our demi-glaces. We roll out our own pasta. We do our own gnocchi. We pair it with whatever happens to be fresh at the farm at the time." Many of the ingredients they use come from his farm twenty-five kilometres away; the rest, especially the seafood, cheese and animal proteins, is sourced from elsewhere on the Island.

In 2020, he opened 10 Acres Café & Market at the Sidney Pier Hotel & Spa, where he also sells preserves and baked goods. "Sidney is actually booming," he says. "There are as many high-end strollers as there are electric scooters." Next, he's planning to build a cidery and distillery at the farm, where he hopes to make eau-de-vie (a colourless fruit brandy) and host tours, tastings and farm lunches. "It's an active 10.014 acres," he says.

Gnocchi with Roasted Squash and Beets

SERVES 2 This gnocchi recipe from 10 Acres Bistro executive chef Marcelo Najarro is one of the restaurant's perennial favourites. His team makes it with a variety of vegetables fresh from the farm, so go ahead and improvise with whatever is in season.

Gnocchi

1¼ lbs starchy potatoes, such as russet or Yukon Gold, unpeeled

1 cup flour, plus extra for dusting

4 egg yolks

Salt, to taste

1 Tbsp canola or olive oil

Roasted beets

2 to 3 golden beets (6 oz), stems trimmed and scrubbed well

Roasted squash

1 butternut squash, peeled, seeded and cut into 1-inch cubes

2 Tbsp olive oil

Salt and black pepper, to taste

Assembly

2 Tbsp butter

1 tsp canola oil

¾ cup Roasted Squash (see here)

¾ cup Roasted Beets (see here)

1 Tbsp finely chopped sage

Salt, to taste

Gnocchi (see here)

Hazelnuts, peeled, lightly toasted and crushed, for garnish

Grated or shaved Parmesan, for garnish

Gnocchi Preheat oven to 400°F.

Pierce potatoes a few times with a fork, then roast in their jackets for 45 minutes, until cooked through.

Remove from oven and, working quickly but carefully, scoop out the potato flesh, and rice it while it is still hot. Transfer riced potatoes to a bowl.

Add flour, egg yolks and a generous pinch of salt to the potatoes. Using your hands, lightly mix until you have a fluffy dough. (It's important to mix by hand, not a machine, to avoid overworking the dough.)

On a lightly floured work surface, roll out dough by hand into a rope with a 1-inch diameter. Cut rope into 1-inch pieces.

Bring a large saucepan of salted water to a boil. Drop gnocchi into the water and cook for 2 to 3 minutes, until they float to the surface. Using a slotted spoon, transfer gnocchi to a bowl. (Don't dump or strain them or they will be crushed!) Add oil, toss gently and set aside to cool.

Roasted beets Preheat oven to 400°F.

Wrap the beets in aluminum foil—wrap bigger ones individually and smaller ones together. Place on a baking sheet and roast for 50 to 60 minutes, until a fork or skewer slides in easily. (Large beets may take a little longer.) Set aside to cool.

Peel the beets—the skin should rub off easily. Then cut into bite-sized pieces.

Roasted squash Preheat oven to 400°F (or add squash to the oven while the beets are roasting).

Combine all ingredients in a large bowl. Arrange on a baking sheet and roast for 25 to 30 minutes, until tender and lightly browned.

Assembly Combine butter and oil in a frying pan over medium-low heat. Add squash and beets and cook for 5 to 10 minutes, until lightly crisp and golden. Stir in sage and season with salt—the butter should turn golden brown, with a rich, nutty aroma.

Add gnocchi and gently sauté for 3 to 5 minutes. Gently swirl the pan to prevent sticking and until ingredients are heated through and some edges are golden brown.

Transfer gnocchi to 2 plates and garnish with crushed hazelnuts and Parmesan.

Tiramisu

MAKES 8 TO 10 (500-ML) JARS This classic Italian recipe is one of the most popular desserts at 10 Acres Bistro. They serve it in individual wide-mouth Mason jars, but feel free to use whatever type of vessel you prefer—you can even present it in a trifle bowl or baking dish.

9 egg yolks

1⅔ cups sugar

1⅔ cups mascarpone, room temperature

2½ cups heavy (36%) cream

1½ tsp vanilla extract

1 cup cold espresso

1 oz Kahlúa

1 oz dark rum

1 to 2 (7-oz) packages ladyfingers, as needed

Cocoa powder, for sprinkling

Prepare an ice bath by filling a large bowl halfway with cold water and ice.

In a medium heatproof bowl, whisk egg yolks with sugar for 5 minutes, until well mixed. Bring a medium saucepan of water to a low simmer, then place the bowl with the egg mixture overtop. Whisk for 12 to 15 minutes, until pale and thick. Remove from heat.

Cover with plastic wrap, pressing film directly onto the surface to prevent a skin from forming. Place the bowl into the ice bath for 20 minutes until cooled to room temperature.

Meanwhile, beat mascarpone in a large mixing bowl until smooth and creamy.

Using a stand mixer fitted with a whisk attachment, whip cream and vanilla at medium-high speed until high peaks form.

Remove the plastic from the egg mixture. Using a silicone spatula, slowly fold the whipped cream, in small batches, into the egg mixture. Then fold this mixture, again in small batches, into the mascarpone.

In a separate bowl, combine espresso, Kahlúa and rum.

Cut ladyfingers into lengths that will fit into the base of the vessel you plan to use. (At 10 Acres, they use 500-mL wide-mouth Mason jars, but you could also use a large bowl.) Quickly dip ladyfingers into the espresso mixture and lay them in one layer. Drizzle a tablespoon of the espresso mixture overtop, then spread with a ½-inch layer of the mascarpone filling. Repeat another 1 to 2 times, ending with the mascarpone mixture. Sprinkle cocoa powder overtop, then chill overnight to allow the flavours and textures to set.

1909 KITCHEN

Terry Somerville and Kristine Morrow

Terry Somerville and Kristine Morrow were living and cooking in Ontario when Tofino Resort + Marina called them west for an opportunity they couldn't resist. "We drove across the country," Somerville says. "We burned rubber and made it to the Island in four days." It was the summer of 2020, and they couldn't wait to settle down somewhere smaller and foodier. "It's a really good career opportunity," Morrow says, "and a really good lifestyle opportunity."

Now the husband-and-wife team is running the kitchen at the marinaside 1909 Kitchen, he as executive chef, she as executive pastry chef. They follow in the footsteps of opening chef Paul Moran, who took his winnings from *Top Chef Canada* to follow his passion and become a full-time forager—he returns occasionally to host Forage and Feast dinners.

Although Somerville and Morrow are both originally from Ontario, they met while working in Vancouver, first at MARKET by Jean-Georges and then Hawksworth Restaurant. "Kristine fell for me at Hawksworth and the rest is history," Somerville says. He went on to open Meat & Bread; she was part of the opening teams at both the Fairmont Pacific Rim and BETA5 Chocolates.

At 1909 Kitchen, named for the year Tofino's first post office opened, they are making things "a little more comfort-driven and classic," Morrow says. She's launching a from-scratch pastry program that will focus on cakes, tortes and ice cream; he's using the wood-fired Mugnaini oven for vegetables, pizza and whole fish. That is, when they are not busy relishing the restaurant's 270-degree views of Clayoquot Sound, savouring the local seafood and wild mushrooms, or chasing after their two young children.

"It's a beautiful place and we are enjoying our time here," Somerville says. "We're making food we love to eat. Getting a really nice atmosphere going. Laughing and having a good time."

Cioppino

SERVES 4 TO 6 Coastal flavours collide in this Tofino seafood stew from chef Terry Somerville at 1909 Kitchen at the Tofino Resort + Marina. You can sear, bake or grill the fish separately from the clams, mussels and prawns—that way, it's less likely to flake into small pieces. Although the charred shellfish stock adds wonderfully complex flavours, you can use a purchased fish stock.

Spice blend

1 Tbsp fennel seeds
2 Tbsp smoked paprika
¼ tsp cayenne pepper

Charred shellfish stock

3 to 4 lemons, halved
1 to 2 jalapeño peppers
2 lbs prawn heads and shells
Olive oil
½ bulb fennel, thinly sliced
2 large onions, thinly sliced
2 stalks celery, thinly sliced
1 large carrot, thinly sliced
1 head garlic, top cut off
2 Tbsp tomato paste
1 cup white wine
1 tsp reserved toasted fennel seeds (from Spice Blend)
6 sprigs thyme
10 sprigs Italian parsley

Cioppino

2 L Charred Shellfish Stock (see here) or fish stock
Olive oil
2 shallots, sliced
½ bulb fennel, thinly sliced
3 cloves garlic, thinly sliced
1 cup cherry tomatoes, halved
2 Tbsp Spice Blend (see here)
Pinch of crushed red pepper
Pinch of saffron
1 lb live clams, scrubbed
1 lb live mussels, scrubbed and debearded
8 fresh large prawns
12 oz ling cod or smoked black cod, cut into bite-sized pieces

½ cup puréed San Marzano tomatoes
½ cup white wine
Salt, to taste
Handful of Italian parsley, chopped
2 green onions, chopped
Good-quality olive oil, for drizzling
Toasted bread, to serve

Spice blend Set a small frying pan over medium-high heat and add fennel seeds. Heat for 2 to 3 minutes, stirring, until fragrant and lightly toasted. Cool, then set 1 teaspoon aside for the stock. Using a mortar and pestle, grind the remaining fennel seeds. Transfer to a small bowl, add paprika and cayenne, and mix well.

Charred shellfish stock Preheat oven to 425°F.

Heat a large cast-iron pan over medium-high heat and char lemons, cut-side down, and jalapeños for 5 minutes. (Alternatively, grill them over a wood or charcoal fire.) Set aside.

On a baking sheet, toss prawn heads and shells in a little oil and roast for 10 to 15 minutes, stirring occasionally. Transfer shells to a stockpot.

Toss sliced vegetables and garlic with a little oil, place on baking sheet and roast for 5 minutes. Stir in tomato paste and roast for another 10 minutes. Pour wine onto baking sheet, scraping up all the caramelized bits, then add vegetables and all the pan scrapings to the stockpot.

Add enough cold water to cover ingredients by 2 inches. Bring to a boil over

high heat, skimming off any scum from the surface. Add reserved fennel seeds, jalapeños (whole, or halved and seeded), 2 charred lemon halves and the herbs and simmer uncovered for 2 to 3 hours.

Strain stock through a fine-mesh sieve over a large bowl or into another saucepan. Using the back of the ladle, crush shells to extract all that lovely stock. Set stock aside and keep warm if using right away. Alternatively, refrigerate for up to 2 days until needed.

Cioppino In a medium saucepan, bring the stock to a simmer and keep hot while you prepare the cioppino. Place a large, heavy-bottomed pot over medium-high heat and add enough oil to coat the bottom. When oil is hot, add shallots, fennel and garlic and cook for 2 to 3 minutes.

Add cherry tomatoes, spice blend, crushed red pepper and saffron and cook for 2 minutes, until fragrant. Add clams, mussels, prawns and fish, then stir to coat.

Pour in puréed tomatoes and wine and increase to high heat. Bring to a boil and add enough hot stock to cover seafood by 1 to 2 inches. Cover and simmer for 3 to 5 minutes until the mussels and clams open and the prawns and fish are just cooked. Discard any unopened clams and mussels.

Remove from heat and stir in parsley and green onions. Season to taste, ladle into bowls and drizzle olive oil overtop. Serve with remaining charred lemon halves and toasted bread.

Double Chocolate Brownie Cookies

MAKES 16 (2-OZ) COOKIES Pastry chef Kristine Morrow's cookies have a soft, chewy centre that will make chocolate lovers swoon. She suggests you make a large batch of the cookie dough, scoop it and freeze the individually scooped portions. Allow frozen cookie dough to come to fridge temperature before baking. This way you can have freshly baked cookies whenever needed.

1½ cups flour

½ cup unsweetened cocoa powder

2 tsp baking powder

½ tsp salt

2 eggs

½ cup unsweetened coconut milk

1 tsp vanilla extract

1⅓ cups dark chocolate chips

½ cup (1 stick) butter, room temperature

1¼ cups lightly packed brown sugar

½ cup milk chocolate chips

Flaked sea salt, for sprinkling (optional)

Sift flour, cocoa powder, baking powder and salt into a large bowl.

In a separate bowl, combine eggs, coconut milk and vanilla. Lightly mix and set aside.

Bring a medium saucepan of water to a simmer over medium heat. Place the dark chocolate chips in a heatproof bowl, then place the bowl over the pot of simmering water to create a double boiler. Stir chocolate until melted and smooth. Remove from heat and set aside to cool.

Using an electric mixer, cream butter and brown sugar together in a large bowl on medium-high speed for 2 minutes, until well combined.

Alternate adding egg mixture and dry ingredients to the butter-sugar mixture, a third at a time, starting with the egg mixture. Mix well, occasionally scraping down the bowl. Add melted chocolate and mix well. Stir in milk chocolate chips and mix until dough is combined. Cover bowl with plastic wrap and refrigerate for at least 1 hour.

Preheat oven to 350°F. Line two baking sheets with parchment paper or silicone mats. Remove dough from the fridge and let sit at room temperature for 5 to 10 minutes.

Using a 2-ounce ice cream scoop, scoop balls of dough onto the prepared baking sheets, evenly spacing them 2 inches apart. Bake cookies for 15 minutes, until edges are set and firm. Sprinkle with flaked sea salt (if using) and set aside to cool completely.

BEACH FIRE BREWING AND NOSH HOUSE

Laura Gosnell

"Beer," says chef Laura Gosnell, "creates a social situation and food is part of that." So when she and business partner Darrin Finnerty opened Beach Fire in Campbell River in 2016, they decided to pay the same attention to the food menu as the beer—something most breweries weren't doing.

Gosnell grew up in the Kootenays and in Port McNeill on northern Vancouver Island, but she spent a number of years travelling and working elsewhere, and that inspired her to do more than typical pub fare. She wanted to offer share plates made from the incredible local products in the area. "The growing season is long here so we can get greens most of the year," Gosnell says. "We have six different farms we deal with. There are local foragers for mushrooms, and commercial fishermen whose families have been here for generations."

And of course Campbell River, which claims the title Salmon Capital of the World, has incredible seafood. "All the seafood we serve is local and we can buy directly from the boats in the harbour," she says. "It's created nice relationships with the other people in the community." Those warm connections grow around the harvest tables and hand-hewn maple bar at Beach Fire, helped by the ever-changing taps of Finnerty's brews.

Everything is made from scratch and the menu changes twice a day. Gosnell is also very focused on sustainability and managing waste.

All her time spent off-island made Gosnell realize something. "We're supplying top-end food to other places in the world and I think some people take our local ingredients for granted," she says. It made her realize something else, too: "It feels like home here."

Chipotle-Lime Mussels

SERVES 2 TO 4 The shellfish from these northern waters are among the best in the world, and Beach Fire makes the most of them in this flavourful dish. Serve with plenty of bread to get every last drop of that irresistible sauce.

1 (186-mL) can chipotle peppers in adobo sauce

2 to 3 cloves garlic

2½ lbs live mussels, scrubbed and debearded

1 Tbsp olive oil

Juice of 1 lime

½ cup heavy (36%) cream

Fresh bread, to serve

In a small food processor, combine chipotle peppers and adobo sauce with garlic and process until smooth. (The paste can be stored in the fridge for up to a month or frozen in ice cube portions for future use. Great for zesting up chilis, salsas or aiolis!)

Put mussels in a colander and rinse under cold running water. Discard any that are open and won't close when tapped or that have broken shells.

Heat oil in a heavy-bottomed frying pan over medium-high heat. Add 2 table-spoons chipotle-garlic paste and sauté for 1 or 2 minutes, until fragrant. Add mussels and increase heat to high. Deglaze with lime juice, then cover and steam for 1 minute.

Add cream and cook for another 2 to 3 minutes, until mussels have opened and mussel liquor reduces. Discard any unopened mussels.

Serve mussels and broth in a shallow bowl with fresh bread for sopping up the sauce.

Double Chocolate Stout Cake

SERVES 12 TO 14 Beer is not just for drinking; it's also for baking into this rich, dark, intensely chocolatey cake from Beach Fire Brewing and Nosh House.

Ganache

2½ cups heavy (36%) cream

2½ cups good-quality dark chocolate chips (at least 60% cacao)

Cake

2 cups (4 sticks) butter, plus extra for greasing

2 cups stout

1½ cups unsweetened cocoa powder (not Dutch process)

4 cups flour

4 cups sugar

1 Tbsp baking soda

1½ tsp salt

4 eggs

1⅓ cups sour cream

Ganache Simmer cream in saucepan over medium heat. Do not scald. Add chocolate chips and whisk for a minute, until melted and smooth. Remove from heat and set aside to cool to room temperature, until ganache has a frosting-like consistency.

Cake Preheat oven to 350°F. Line the bottoms of 2 10-inch springform pans with parchment paper and grease the paper and the sides.

Combine butter and stout in a saucepan and cook over medium heat until butter has melted. Whisk in cocoa powder, then set aside to cool.

Using a stand or handheld mixer, whisk together the flour, sugar, baking soda and salt on low speed until evenly incorporated.

In a separate large bowl, whisk together eggs and sour cream, then slowly mix in the cooled stout mixture. Add wet ingredients to the dry ingredients and run on low until well combined. Scrape bowl and mix at medium-high for 2 minutes.

Divide batter evenly between the springform pans. Bake for 60 to 75 minutes, checking after 50 minutes, until a toothpick inserted into the centre of the cake comes out clean. Set aside to cool.

Remove cakes from springform pans, but keep them on the parchment until you are ready to layer them. (It makes them much easier to handle.)

Place one cake upside-down on a cake plate and remove the parchment. Liberally spread ganache over the cake. Remove parchment from the second cake and place it on top of the first, this time right side up. Starting from the centre, spread ganache over the cake, then down the sides. Turn the cake plate as you work so that the cake is covered all around in an even layer of ganache.

Serve at room temperature or refrigerate until needed.

Note: If your kitchen is too warm, allow ganache to cool to room temperature then place the bowl in an ice bath. Whisk constantly until the desired texture is achieved. (It should hold its shape on the whisk.)

BLUE SPRUCE ICE CREAM

Kirsten Wood

Who doesn't love ice cream? Especially when it's as luxuriously rich and brightly flavoured as the ice cream Kirsten Wood offers? "Everyone is happy when they come in," says the owner of Blue Spruce Ice Cream in downtown Courtenay. "It's amazing."

Mind you, making ice cream wasn't her first career goal. Born in Cumberland to a Saddle Lake Cree family originally from central Alberta, Wood moved to Vancouver to study music and First Nations political science, then lived in the U.S. "playing music and adventuring." When her dad had a heart attack back home, it really hit her hard: "I asked myself, 'What are you doing?' I needed to be with my family." But as Wood says, "It was always in my plan to move back. I always wanted to open up a store and be part of the downtown community. There was nothing similar and it gave me an opportunity to do something that complemented our downtown."

At Blue Spruce, she and her all-female team, including baker Katelyn Penner, make almost everything from scratch, even the sprinkles, and as much of it as possible from local ingredients such as berries, herbs, eggs, spruce tips and even Meyer lemons from Innisfree Farm in Royston. "There are no shortcuts," Wood says. "We get our milk from Morningstar Farm where it's nice to visit the cows and dogs. We also get bull kelp from Salish Seas Products on Cortes Island. And we do a water buffalo yogurt with quince that I love. But our signature ice cream is our spruce tip ice cream."

One of her most popular items is a bannock ice cream sandwich that is a nod to her First Nations background. Though to be sure, she says, "We're using local and traditionally Indigenous ingredients that have become mainstream. The two are so linked."

Spiked Spruce Float

SERVES 1   This heady, herbaceous Blue Spruce Ice Cream cocktail, created with bartender Brian Chapman of My Teacher Drinks, is a spirited float inspired by a classic Negroni.

2 oz melted Spruce Tip Ice Cream (page 32)

1 oz gin (preferably Sheringham Kazuki)

¾ oz Campari

2 small scoops Spruce Tip Ice Cream (page 32)

Strawberry slice, mint leaf and/or spruce bud, for garnish

In a shaker tin, combine melted ice cream, gin, Campari and some ice. Shake, shake, shake!

Place scooped ice cream into a Collins glass. Strain cocktail overtop. Garnish with a strawberry slice and a mint leaf or, if you prefer, a spruce bud. Serve with a long spoon.

Bannock Ice Cream Sandwich

Kirsten Wood infuses this sweet treat with both indigenous ingredients and the traditions of her Indigenous family. Bannock, also known as fry bread, envelops her signature spruce tip ice cream, made from the tender new growth that appears in spring. Note that agar agar, which is made from seaweed, is used to thicken and stabilize ice cream; it is optional but can improve the texture noticeably.

Spruce tip ice cream

5½ cups milk

2½ cups whipping (33%)
   cream

⅓ cup skim milk powder

½ cup finely chopped spruce
   tips (divided) (see Note)

2 tsp agar agar (optional)

½ tsp sea salt

2 cups sugar

¾ cup egg yolks
   (10 to 12 eggs)

Strawberry sauce

2 lbs fresh or frozen
   strawberries

½ cup sugar

1 Tbsp lemon juice

Cinnamon sugar

½ cup sugar

2 Tbsp ground cinnamon

Assembly

Whipping (33%) cream,
   to taste

Spruce tip ice cream Freeze your ice cream bowl if using a household ice cream maker.

Create an ice bath in a large bowl or your kitchen sink.

In a large saucepan, combine milk and cream and stir frequently over medium-low heat until it reaches a temperature of 120°F. Add skim milk powder, half of the spruce tips, agar agar (if using) and salt. Stir until well combined and slowly bring to a temperature of 140°F.

Mix together the sugar and egg yolks using a stand or handheld mixer, until just combined. Work quickly, but take care not to add too much air. Slowly and gradually add about ½ cup of the hot milk mixture into the eggs, adding just a little at a time, to temper it.

Pour the tempered egg mixture into the rest of the milk mixture. Cook over medium heat, stirring constantly, until the custard reaches 175°F. Strain through a fine-mesh sieve into a large bowl to remove any solids. Stir in remaining spruce tips and place the bowl into the ice bath, taking care not to add water to your custard!

Stir custard often until it's cooled to room temperature. Pour cooled custard into an ice cream maker and freeze according to the manufacturer's instructions.

Strawberry sauce Combine all ingredients in a saucepan over medium-high heat. Bring to a boil, then reduce heat to medium and cook until strawberries are soft and mixture is foaming. Turn off heat and set aside to cool slightly.

Using an immersion blender, blend until smooth. Strain through a fine-mesh sieve to remove seeds, if desired. Place sauce in a container and chill completely.

Cinnamon sugar Combine sugar and cinnamon in a bowl large enough for tossing the pieces of bannock. Set aside.

Fried bannock In a large bowl, combine flour, baking powder, sugar and salt. Make a well, add milk (or water) and mix until a dough starts to form. If it doesn't come together or feels too dry, add more liquid. Slowly add melted butter and knead until dough is smooth. Set aside to rest for 10 to 15 minutes.

Roll dough out into a rectangle, ¼ inch thick. Let sit for 2 to 3 minutes, then cut into 4-inch rounds (or squares) as evenly as possible.

Pour oil into a deep fryer or deep saucepan and heat to a temperature of 350°F. Working in batches, carefully lower dough into the pan, taking care not to splash hot oil. Deep-fry for 8 minutes, turning occasionally, until golden and puffy on both sides. Using a slotted spoon, transfer bannock to a paper towel–lined rack to drain. Cool slightly. Repeat with remaining pieces.

Assembly Place bannock in the bowl of cinnamon sugar and toss well. To serve, cut each piece open like a pita and fill with ice cream, whipped cream and strawberry sauce.

Note: Sitka spruce trees bud April to May on the West Coast. If you're looking to harvest spruce buds yourself, be sure to identify them correctly (they look similar to hemlock and other tree buds) and harvest only the bright green new growth. Clean thoroughly before use. If not used fresh, they can be frozen in an airtight container or dehydrated and turned into a powder.

Fried bannock

3 cups flour

3 Tbsp baking powder

1 Tbsp sugar

½ tsp salt

¾ milk or water, plus extra if needed

½ cup (1 stick) butter, melted

Canola oil, for deep-frying

Cinnamon sugar (see here)

BOOM + BATTEN

Matt Cusano

The elevated casual Boom + Batten is located in Victoria's Songhees district, quite literally on the Inner Harbour—a kayak pathway flows right under the 6,900-square-foot restaurant and café. "We have a big, beautiful bar and every seat in the restaurant has a water view," says managing partner Paul Simpson. "We have Harbour Air seaplanes taking off and landing in front of us. Every day, guests and staff see amazing sea life and lots of harbour activity: sea lions, otters, kayakers and luxury yachts."

Boom + Batten opened in June 2019, as part of the new Victoria International Marina, Canada's first mega yacht marina. It's not just the otters and kayakers that pass by. "Hundreds and hundreds of people walk by every day on the Songhees Walkway," Simpson says, so a café serving fresh-baked goods made in-house is a major part of their success.

But the main focus is on chef Matt Cusano's all-encompassing menu, which is heavily influenced by his Italian heritage. "We have an extensive steak list, a full forno oven for flatbreads and pizzas and a wide variety of seafood including Humboldt squid, tuna, shellfish and sablefish. We have a really diverse menu that has something for everybody," Cusano says.

Originally from Calgary, Cusano arrived in Victoria by way of the Okanagan where he worked at Quails' Gate Estate Winery under chef Roger

Sleiman, who he calls "the godfather of farm-to-table dining in the Okanagan." Now, with all of Vancouver Island's produce to use, he couldn't be happier. "Top ingredients and unique culinary experiences are something Victoria customers are looking for," he says. "I love my surroundings and Victoria—I will be here for a long time."

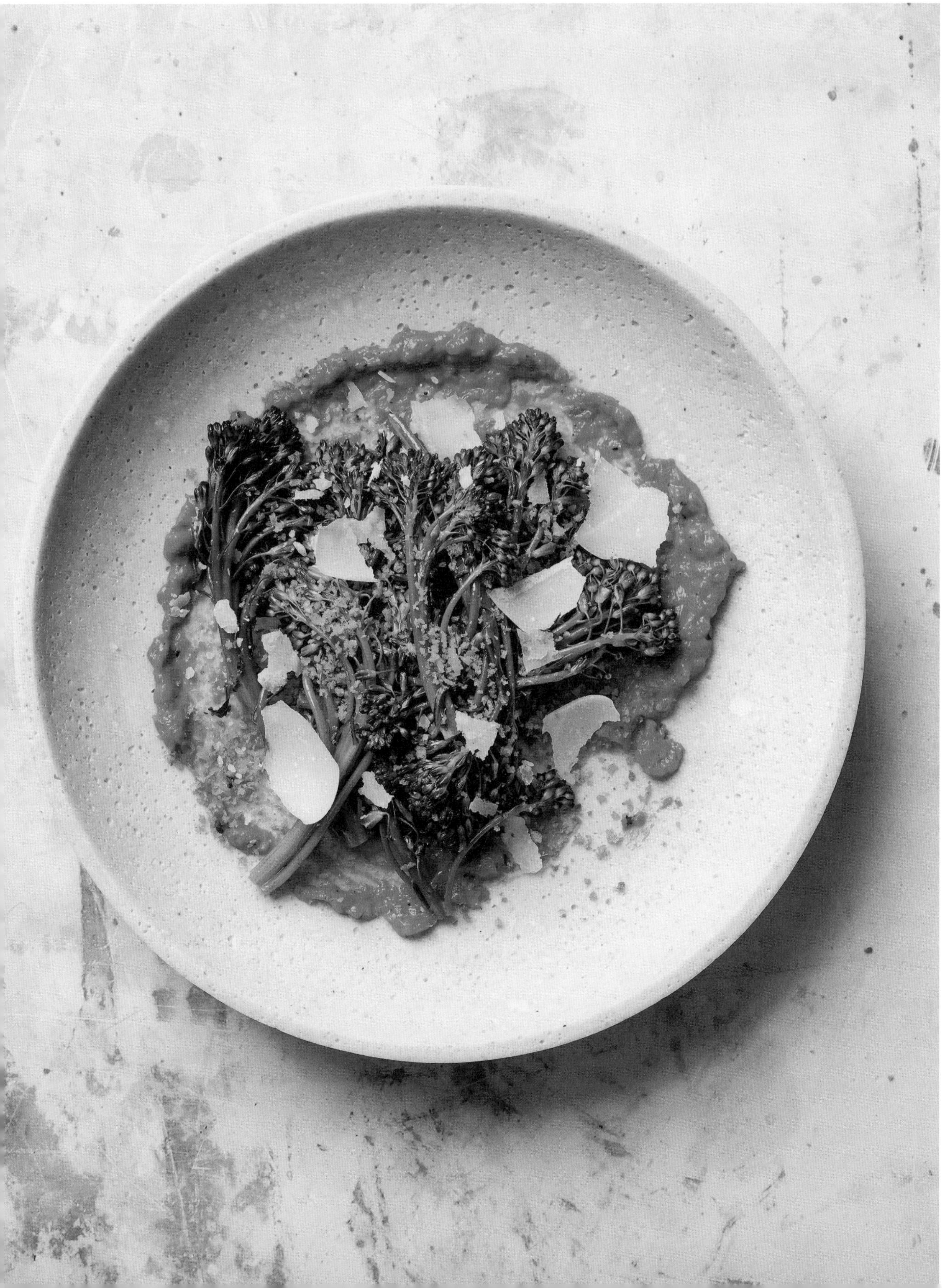

Roasted Broccolini with Romesco Sauce and Pecorino p. 36

Roasted Broccolini with Romesco Sauce and Pecorino

SERVES 4 (AS A SIDE DISH) The roasted broccolini from Boom + Batten's Matt Cusano is delicious on its own, but the tangy romesco sauce puts it over the top. Great served as an appetizer or as a side to steak, chicken, fish—just about anything.

Romesco sauce

2 red bell peppers
2 Roma tomatoes, halved
1 shallot, chopped
1 clove garlic
¼ cup shelled pumpkin seeds
1 Tbsp smoked paprika
1 Tbsp sugar
1 Tbsp salt
¼ tsp black pepper
½ cup extra-virgin olive oil
2 Tbsp sherry vinegar

Roasted broccolini

2 lbs broccolini, ends trimmed
6 Tbsp olive oil (divided)
Salt and black pepper, to taste
1 clove garlic, finely chopped
Sprig of thyme, leaves picked and chopped
½ cup panko crumbs
¼ tsp smoked paprika
Grated zest of ½ lemon

Assembly

1 cup shaved Pecorino Romano

Romesco sauce Preheat oven to 450°F.

Place red peppers and tomatoes on a baking sheet and roast for 20 minutes, until peppers are blistered and dark.

Place peppers in a bowl and cover tightly with plastic wrap. Place tomato halves in a separate bowl, uncovered, and set aside to cool. Reserve any pan juices.

Gently remove tomato skin and discard. Repeat with red peppers, and then remove the stems and seeds. Roughly chop tomatoes. Again, reserve any juices.

In a blender, combine tomatoes and peppers, with any reserved juices, and the remaining ingredients. Blend on high until smooth. Set sauce aside.

Roasted broccolini Preheat oven to 450°F.

In a large bowl, combine broccolini, ¼ cup oil and salt and pepper. Toss well, then space out in a single layer on a baking sheet and roast for 15 minutes, until tender.

Heat the remaining 2 tablespoons oil in a small frying pan over medium heat. Add garlic and thyme and sauté for 1 minute, then stir in panko crumbs and paprika. Season with salt and pepper. Sauté for 2 to 3 minutes, until panko crumbs turn light brown. Transfer mixture to a bowl, add lemon zest and stir.

Assembly Spoon a generous amount of romesco sauce onto the centre of each plate and use the back of the spoon to spread evenly in a circle. Stack broccolini high on the plate, then sprinkle Pecorino Romano and toasted panko overtop.

Spaghetti alle Vongole (Spaghetti with Clams)

SERVES 4 The waters around Vancouver Island are abundant with shellfish, both wild and farmed, including several types of clams: razor clams, butter clams, littleneck clams and Manila clams. Sweetly briny and toothsomely tender, any of them would be delicious in this classic pasta dish from Boom + Batten.

1 (450-g) package dried spaghetti

¼ cup extra-virgin olive oil

2 shallots, finely chopped

2 cloves garlic, finely chopped

1 tsp crushed red pepper

3 oz pancetta, diced

1½ lbs Manila clams, cleaned

¾ cup white wine

½ cup chopped Italian parsley, plus extra for garnish

¼ cup (½ stick) butter

Juice of 1 lemon

½ tsp black pepper

Italian parsley (optional)

Parmesan, for garnish (optional)

Bring a large pot of salted water to a rolling boil. Add spaghetti and stir to prevent clumps. Cook for 8 to 10 minutes, until pasta is al dente. Drain, reserving ½ cup of pasta water.

Heat oil in a large frying pan over medium heat. Add shallots, garlic and crushed red pepper. Sauté for 3 minutes, until shallots are light brown and translucent. Stir in pancetta and sauté for another minute, until slightly rendered.

Add clams and stir well. Increase heat to high and cook for a minute, keeping the pan moving. Add wine and cook for another minute, then cover and reduce heat to medium. Steam clams for 5 to 10 minutes, until they open. Discard any unopened clams.

Add cooked pasta, parsley, butter and lemon juice and cook for another 1 to 3 minutes until the sauce is slightly reduced. Season with black pepper. If the sauce is too thick, thin out with a little reserved pasta water.

Divide pasta among 4 bowls, then top with clams and sauce. Garnish with parsley and Parmesan (if using).

BRAVOCADOS

David Thielmann

David Thielmann can thank "the housing gods of Tofino" for his role as chef-owner of the village's only vegan restaurant.

In 2017, he was at loose ends after cooking at establishments including Victoria's Strathcona Hotel and Vancouver's CinCin Ristorante. Then Colin Minions gave him a call. They'd met back in 2000, when Thielmann was cooking at Mission Springs Brewing Company. Now Minions was asking him to take over the kitchen at his vegetarian restaurant in Tofino. Thielmann was undecided, until he saw the suite upstairs. "It was the most beautiful apartment I'd ever seen in my life and I said, 'Now I'm interested.'"

He himself was moving toward a plant-based diet—he calls himself a "veggan," a vegan who eats eggs—and was grateful to inherit a loyal team, including sous chef and front of house manager Lise Richard. But he was also executive chef at a restaurant in Port Alberni, splitting his time and energy between them, and getting, he says, "a little burnt out." It didn't help that he had to move out of the "penthouse" and into a trailer, then a temporary apartment rental. Then Bravocados came up for sale at the same time the lease on his apartment expired. Luckily, those fickle housing gods were smiling once again, and he found a place to live just in time. "I've always loved Tofino and I love Bravocados," he says.

The restaurant is now fully vegan, well known for dishes like the killer faux "fysh & chips," made from sea-brined, panko-crusted banana blossom. Thielmann is building a backyard bistro, perfecting his black bean Bravo Burger and regularly switching up his menu "to keep it interesting for staff and customers as well." And Bravocados has become a mainstay for locals and visitors alike. "I'm not changing the philosophy of the restaurant," he says. "People love it."

Vegan Caesar Cocktail

SERVES 1 At Bravocados, a versatile sea brine is chef-owner Dave Thielmann's foundation for several vegan dishes—he uses it in his oyster mushroom "scallops" and "calamari," his banana blossom "fysh & chips" and his heart of palm chowder. But its best use is surely in this vegan Caesar cocktail. Keep a batch of the base in your fridge (it'll last up to three weeks at least) and serve as needed with a shot of vodka, gin or tequila.

Sea brine

2 litres water
1 lemon, halved
2 to 3 cloves garlic, crushed
2 nori sheets or equivalent in dried kelp
2 Tbsp sea salt

Cocktail base

1 (1.89-L) jug Mott's Garden Cocktail Juice
Juice of 3 to 4 limes
1 cup pickle juice
1 cup Sea Brine (see here)
¼ cup horseradish
¼ cup vegan Worcestershire sauce
Tabasco sauce or any other hot sauce, to taste

Vegan Caesar

1 lime wedge
Celery salt or other seasoned salt, for rim (optional)
Ice cubes
4 oz Cocktail Base (see here)
1 to 2 oz vodka, gin or tequila
Spicy pickled beans, celery spears, skewered olives, pickled asparagus or other aromatic vegetable, for garnish (optional)

Sea brine Combine all ingredients in a large pot and boil for 30 minutes. Strain, then set aside to cool. (Nori, or kelp, can be reserved for another use. Brine can be stored in the fridge for up to 3 weeks.)

Cocktail base Combine all ingredients in a large bowl. Adjust seasonings to taste. Pour mixture into a large jug and keep chilled until ready to use. (Cocktail base can be stored in the fridge for up to 3 weeks.)

Vegan Caesar Run the lime wedge around the rim of a pint or highball glass, then dip the rim into a saucer of seasoned salt (if using). Add several ice cubes to the glass.

Pour in cocktail base and vodka, gin or tequila and stir gently. Add garnishes of your choice (if using).

Vegan Apple Pie Waffles

SERVES 6 TO 8 Sweet and hearty, the waffles at Bravocados are topped with a spiced apple compote and coconut cream, creating a brunch dish that will satisfy everyone around the table.

Whipped coconut cream

- 1 (398-mL) can coconut cream, refrigerated upside-down overnight or at least 4 hours (see Notes)
- 2 Tbsp icing sugar
- ½ tsp vanilla extract

Apple pie compote

- 6 apples of your choice, peeled, cored and cut into ½-inch cubes
- ½ cup packed brown sugar
- 1 tsp ground cinnamon
- ¼ tsp ground nutmeg
- ¼ tsp ground cloves
- ½ cup + 1 tsp water (divided)
- 2 tsp cornstarch
- 2 Tbsp vegan butter

Waffle batter

- Vegan butter, for greasing
- 1 ripe banana, mashed
- 3 cups oat milk, plus extra if needed
- ½ cup olive oil
- 2 tsp vanilla extract
- 1 tsp maple syrup, plus extra for serving
- 4 cups gluten-free flour, such as Bob's Red Mill, plus extra if needed
- 2 Tbsp baking powder
- ½ tsp salt

Whipped coconut cream Chill a metal bowl and a whisk in the freezer for at least 15 minutes.

Drain the coconut cream by tipping out the water, which will have separated from the now solid cream.

In the chilled bowl, combine the cold coconut cream with the icing sugar and vanilla and whisk slowly, until smooth (do not overmix). Transfer to a covered container and refrigerate until set.

Apple pie compote In a medium saucepan, combine apples, sugar, spices and the ½ cup water. Cook over medium heat for 5 to 10 minutes, until water has cooked out and apples are tender but not mushy.

In a small bowl, combine cornstarch and the 1 teaspoon water and mix well. Add to pan and stir until thickened. Stir in vegan butter, then set aside and keep warm.

Note: When coconut cream is chilled, it solidifies and separates from the water. Placing it upside down in the fridge makes it easy to pour the water off and use the cream.

Waffle batter Preheat waffle maker and brush liberally with vegan butter.

In a large bowl, mash banana. Whisk in milk, oil, vanilla and syrup.

In another bowl, sift together flour, baking powder and salt. Make a well in the centre and pour in wet ingredients. Mix well. It's okay if the batter is a bit lumpy, but it shouldn't be thick and clumpy, or thin and runny. Add more oat milk or flour if needed.

Pour batter into waffle maker and cook for 5 minutes, until golden brown.

Plate waffles and top with warm apple pie compote, whipped coconut cream and maple syrup.

Note: Coconut cream and coconut milk are two different products with different uses—coconut cream is much thicker and richer than coconut milk, and contains about four times as much coconut.

BRENTWOOD BAY RESORT

Cooper Green

It's just a twenty-minute drive from downtown Victoria, but Brentwood Bay Resort could be in another world. Perched amid the trees above a marina and with glorious views of the bay, the resort will have you feeling cared for and rested the moment you arrive.

It's a popular spot with visitors as well as locals who enjoy casual fare in the resort's pub and celebrate special occasions in the elegantly relaxed Arbutus Room. Both venues feature live music throughout the weekend. And cooking up the resort's bright, seasonal fare is chef Cooper Green, who joined the team in late 2019, after cooking for twenty years in Vancouver, Victoria, Thailand and Australia.

"I moved to the Island because my wife is from here," says Green. "We wanted a slower pace of life after living in Vancouver. It just felt like the right place to raise our family." What he fell in love with instantly was the incredible produce of the peninsula. "The Saanich Peninsula has farms everywhere," he says. "We're trying to be as local as possible in the Arbutus Room. We take a lot of care with the preparations. It's a great place to be for local ingredients."

Everything possible is made in-house, and he's revised the dining experience to be a little more casual and a little more shareable, especially in the pub. He's also brought in a lighter, more modern style of cooking, adding Asian flavours to dishes like the chili squid. "We want to take pub food to the next level by putting a little twist on the classics to make them special."

Crispy Chili Squid

SERVES 4 This dish is a new take on your average pub-style calamari. At Brentwood Bay's pub, it's made with fresh ingredients, simple techniques and just a little kick of heat.

Chili mayonnaise

1 Tbsp sambal oelek (Indonesian garlic chili paste)

¼ cup mayonnaise

Juice of 1 lime

Crispy chili squid

4 cups canola oil, for deep-frying

4 cloves garlic, finely chopped

3 green onions, finely chopped

1 yellow onion, finely chopped

1 jalapeño pepper, seeded and finely chopped

1 (1-inch) piece of ginger, peeled and finely chopped

Bunch of cilantro, coarsely chopped

6 large (U-5) squid tubes, cleaned and thawed if frozen

1 egg, lightly beaten

1 cup cornstarch

1 Tbsp canola oil

2 Tbsp sambal oelek

Pinch of sea salt

1 lime, cut into wedges, to serve

Chili mayonnaise In a small bowl, combine all ingredients and mix well. Set aside.

Crispy chili squid Pour the 4 cups oil into a deep fryer or deep saucepan and heat to a temperature of 375°F. Line a plate with paper towel.

In a bowl, combine garlic, onions, jalapeño, ginger and cilantro and set aside.

Cut squid tubes in half lengthwise then turn the inside of the tubes to face upwards and scrape flesh with a knife to remove any small pieces of cartilage. Lightly score squid on an angle, cutting just into the flesh to make small crosses. (This will tenderize the squid and help it curl up after it's been fried.) Cut each half tube into triangles—you should have 4 pieces for each half tube.

In a small bowl, combine egg and squid and mix well. Add cornstarch and toss to evenly coat squid.

Heat the 1 tablespoon of oil in a frying pan or wok over medium-high heat. Add onion mixture and sauté for 2 to 3 minutes, until it starts to colour. Add sambal oelek and sauté for another minute. Reduce heat to low.

Carefully lower squid into the deep fryer (or saucepan), taking care not to splash hot oil. Using a slotted spoon or tongs, carefully stir to separate squid. Deep-fry for 1 minute, until squid is light golden brown. Using the slotted spoon (or tongs), transfer squid to the paper towel–lined plate to drain.

Heat the frying pan or wok over high heat to get the onion mixture hot. Add squid, toss well and sprinkle with salt. Pile high on a platter and serve with lime wedges and chili mayonnaise.

Charred Kale and Citrus Salad

SERVES 4 | Charring the kale leaves adds a whole other dimension to the flavour of this salad from Brentwood Bay's chef Cooper Green. It's great for sharing.

Sunflower seed vinaigrette

¾ cup raw sunflower seeds or sunflower seed butter

2 cloves garlic

½ bunch cilantro

¼ cup rice vinegar

Salt

¼ cup water

½ cup olive oil

Salad

2 bunches kale, leaves only

2 Tbsp olive oil

Sea salt

2 Tbsp canola oil

2 shallots, thinly sliced

2 Tbsp cornstarch

Sunflower Seed Vinaigrette (see here)

2 navel oranges, skin and pith removed, segmented

2 grapefruits, skin and pith removed, segmented

¼ cup shelled pumpkin seeds, toasted

Sunflower seed vinaigrette In a blender or food processor, combine sunflower seeds (or sunflower seed butter), garlic, cilantro, rice vinegar, a pinch of salt and ¼ cup water. Blend on high for 30 seconds, then gradually pour in oil and blend until emulsified. It should have a ketchup-like consistency. If necessary, thin out with a little water. Adjust seasoning to taste and set aside.

Salad Preheat a gas or electric grill over high heat

In a large bowl, combine kale, olive oil and a pinch of salt. Place kale on the grill and move leaves around every 20 seconds, until charred along the edges. Transfer to a bowl and set aside.

Heat canola oil in a small frying pan over medium heat. In a small bowl, toss shallots in cornstarch, then add to the pan and sauté for 30 seconds until golden and crispy. Transfer shallots to a paper towel–lined plate to drain, then sprinkle with salt.

Arrange charred kale on a platter and drizzle vinaigrette overtop. Arrange citrus segments on salad, then sprinkle pumpkin seeds and crispy shallots on top, making sure everything is spread out evenly. Finish with sea salt.

BRIE & BARREL

Brad Wutke

Chef Brad Wutke is happy to be back home in Port Alberni. "It's full cycle," he says. "It feels good. There are so many new things going on, so many new businesses." After a decade that saw him graduate from cooking school in Victoria, escape the nuclear disaster in Fukushima, Japan, and spend eight years in remote Arctic communities as an air traffic communicator and weather observer for Environment Canada, he returned to his home-town in June 2019. "I came into Brie & Barrel for my wedding anniversary in August and then it was, 'Aha! I have to work here.'" The very next day he replied to the restaurant's help-wanted ad.

Brie & Barrel is an Italian-style wine bar opened in 2019 by Sharie Minions, the busy mayor of Port Alberni, with chef Dave Thielmann at the helm. When Thielmann left to take ownership of Bravo-cados in Tofino (page 38), Wutke stepped into his executive chef role. "It's definitely the best restau-rant in town, but I'm a little bit biased," he says with a laugh. Brie & Barrel serves pastas, salads and a B.C.-led wine list from a former shoe store that's been given a rustic-elegant makeover. It is located in an up-and-coming part of a town undergoing a major transition, and key to that transition is food, from the cluster of new breweries in town to the local farmers' collective. "There's a lot of people who are motivated to make positive change," Wutke says.

He, too, is planning some changes—for instance, making the menu more eclectic and small plates focused—but with a young family to raise, moving again isn't one of them. "It's going to be awesome," he says happily.

Scallop Potato Salad

SERVES 4 Potato salad is among the humblest of sides. Scallops are among the most luxurious of seafoods. The latter are also enjoying a moment of popularity thanks to new scallop farms along the coast. At Brie & Barrel, the two come together in an easy and impressive dinner party dish. Note that "10/20 size" reflects the number of scallops per pound; however, local scallops may be smaller.

Potato salad

1½ lbs baby potatoes (preferably tricolour)

2 to 3 sprigs thyme + 1 tsp chopped thyme leaves (divided)

1 cup mayonnaise

1 tsp Dijon mustard

2 tsp chopped Italian parsley

1 tsp chopped rosemary

¼ cup chopped green onions

½ bulb fennel, thinly sliced

½ small red onion, finely chopped

¼ stalk celery, finely chopped

Grated zest and juice of 1 lemon

Salt and black pepper, to taste

Scallops

2 Tbsp olive oil

12 to 16 (10/20 size) fresh scallops, muscle removed

Salt

2 Tbsp butter

2 Tbsp capers

Juice of 1 lemon

1 large link dry-cured chorizo, diced

Pickled mustard seeds, celery leaves and/or fennel fronds, for garnish

Potato salad Place baby potatoes and thyme sprigs in a pot of salted water. Bring to a boil, then reduce heat to medium-high and cook for 8 to 10 minutes until fork tender. Strain potatoes and discard thyme sprigs. Set aside to cool to room temperature. Cut into quarters.

In a large bowl, combine mayonnaise, Dijon, parsley, rosemary and remaining 1 teaspoon of thyme. Stir in green onions, fennel, red onions and celery, then add the lemon zest and juice. Add the cooled potatoes to the bowl and mix. Season with salt and pepper.

Scallops Heat oil in a very large non-stick frying pan over medium heat. Pat scallops dry, season with salt, then immediately arrange them in the pan, going clockwise from 12 o'clock. Sear for 1 to 2 minutes until golden brown. Gently flip scallops in the order they were placed in the pan. Sear for another minute.

Quickly add butter, capers, lemon juice and chorizo. Using a large spoon, baste sauce over scallops for another minute, until they are opaque and spring back when gently pressed. Do not overcook.

Transfer potato salad to a large platter or divide between 4 plates or shallow bowls. Arrange scallops on top and spoon capers and chorizo overtop. Drizzle with buttery sauce, then garnish with pickled mustard seeds, celery leaves and/or fennel fronds.

Stilton Cheesecake with Strawberry-Basil Compote

SERVES 12 The combination of sweet and savoury makes for a richly sophisticated dessert at Brie & Barrel. Serve this with a glass of port.

Strawberry-basil compote

2 cups fresh or frozen strawberries, thawed if frozen

½ cup basil leaves and stems (4 oz), plus 12 leaves for garnish

2 Tbsp sugar

2 Tbsp lemon juice

1 Tbsp aged balsamic vinegar (preferably 20-year-old)

½ tsp black pepper

Cheesecake

1 cup graham cracker crumbs

1 cup hazelnuts, half coarsely chopped and half ground (divided)

1 cup + 2 Tbsp sugar (divided)

⅓ cup (⅔ stick) butter, melted, plus extra for greasing

4 (250-g) packages cream cheese, room temperature

4 oz Stilton blue cheese, room temperature

1 cup sour cream, room temperature

2 tsp vanilla extract

3 eggs

⅓ cup flour

Strawberry-basil compote In a saucepan, combine strawberries, basil and sugar and cook over low heat for 10 to 15 minutes. Stir in lemon juice, balsamic and pepper. Remove basil and set aside.

Cheesecake Preheat oven to 350°F. Grease a 10-inch springform pan. Cut a long, skinny piece of parchment paper to line the sides of the pan.

In a bowl, combine graham crumbs, ground hazelnuts, 2 tablespoons sugar and butter and mix well. Transfer mixture to the prepared pan and press into the bottom. Bake for 8 to 10 minutes, until golden. Set aside to cool.

Reduce oven heat to 300°F. Place a pan with a few inches of water in it on the bottom rack to keep the oven moist.

Use a hand mixer to combine cream cheese, blue cheese, sour cream and remaining 1 cup sugar and mix on low speed. Add vanilla, then mix on medium speed for 1 to 2 minutes until smooth. Add an egg, then a third of the flour. Repeat two more times while mixing for 4 to 5 minutes, until smooth (do not overmix).

Pour into the springform pan and smooth out with a spatula. Place cheesecake on the middle rack, centred in the oven, and bake for 1½ hours. Give the pan a gentle shake to see if it's done—the centre should be solid but just slightly wobbly. Bake longer if needed.

Turn off oven and leave door slightly open (use a spoon to prop it), and let cheesecake cool for 1 hour. Move cheesecake from the oven to a rack and cool for another 30 minutes. Refrigerate for 2 to 3 hours.

Cut into slices and plate. Drizzle with strawberry-basil compote, then sprinkle chopped hazelnuts overtop and garnish with basil.

THE BUTCHART GARDENS

Travis Hansen and team

There is perhaps no more iconic attraction on Vancouver Island than The Butchart Gardens. In 1906, Jennie Butchart began transforming her family's limestone quarry by planting a Japanese garden in it. Today it is a vast and beautiful show garden covering fifty-five verdant acres.

So enraptured might you be by the heady aroma of heritage roses or the allure of the elusive Himalayan blue poppies that you might not realize that the food served in the historic family dining room is just as impressive. Leading the culinary program is executive chef Travis Hansen, who has been there for twenty-seven years.

"I'm lucky to look out my kitchen window into one of the most beautiful gardens in the world," he says. "Our food services team is a part of a big family that works together to create these amazing experiences for our guests. We share the same passion and sense of ownership that generations have before us. It's great when we hear stories from our guests, how they visited when they were kids and now they are back with their children—it's full circle."

Not surprisingly, afternoon tea is a popular attraction, as are holiday special events. Edible flowers and herbs from the kitchen gardens feature heavily, whether infusing vinegar or scattered over a salad. "And what we can't grow on the property, we source from local farmers," Hansen says. "We're spoiled. It's literally in our backyard. It's a weird little microclimate here. You can grow everything here. We're showcasing wild, showcasing local, showcasing seasonal."

There are three main outlets here—the Coffee Shop, Blue Poppy Restaurant and upscale Dining Room—as well as the seasonal Gelateria and Annabelle's Café. Almost everything is made from scratch in-house, including well over a dozen flavours of gelato and sorbetto.

As Hansen says, "The garden is the crown jewel, but we want to make sure that you take away a memorable dining experience."

Okanagan Cherry Panzanella

SERVES 4 This bread salad from The Butchart Gardens' executive chef Travis Hansen makes the most of seasonal ingredients—here it's cherries from the Okanagan Valley, a highlight of every summer, but you could use tomatoes, peaches or even cooked peppers. He also includes nasturtium leaves from the kitchen garden. The kitchen makes their own sourdough bread, but a quality store-bought bread would be just fine.

Salted cucumbers

4 Persian cucumbers or
  1 English cucumber, sliced
  into ⅛-inch rounds
2 tsp salt

Macerated summer cherries

6 Tbsp wildflower honey
¼ cup champagne vinegar
¼ cup pink peppercorns,
  coarsely ground
1 lb summer cherries, pitted
  and with stems left on if
  possible (see Note)

Malt vinegar emulsion

1 egg yolk
1 tsp dry mustard
2 Tbsp malt vinegar
½ cup grapeseed oil
Salt, to taste

Assembly

1 loaf sourdough bread, torn
  into bite-sized pieces
3 Tbsp olive oil (divided)
Salt, to taste
4 to 5 French breakfast
  radishes, thinly sliced
1 bulb fennel, thinly sliced
Salted Cucumbers (see here)
Malt Vinegar Emulsion
  (see here)
Macerated Summer Cherries
  (see here)
4 oz blue cheese (preferably
  Poplar Grove Tiger Blue),
  crumbled
2 Tbsp black peppercorns
  (preferably Tellicherry),
  lightly toasted and cracked
24 nasturtium leaves

Salted cucumbers In a bowl, combine cucumbers and salt and lightly toss. Set aside for at least 2 hours to draw out water. Rinse under cold running water and pat dry.

Macerated summer cherries In a medium bowl, whisk together honey, vinegar and peppercorns. Add cherries and let sit at room temperature to macerate for 20 to 30 minutes. Refrigerate until needed.

Malt vinegar emulsion In a small bowl, whisk together egg yolk and dry mustard. Whisk in vinegar. Gradually add oil, a few drops at a time, until liquid thickens. Whisk until emulsified. Season to taste.

Assembly Preheat grill over medium-high heat.

In a large bowl, toss together bread, 2 tablespoons oil and salt. Place on the grill and toast for 1 or 2 minutes on each side, until golden brown and a little charred. (Alternatively, toast under the broiler in your oven for a few minutes, turning to avoid burning too much.) Return bread to the bowl.

Add radishes, fennel and salted cucumbers. Add remaining tablespoon of oil and toss well. Adjust seasoning to taste.

Spoon salad onto a large platter. Drizzle with the malt vinegar emulsion, then top with summer cherries, blue cheese, peppercorns and nasturtium leaves.

Note: If you don't have a cherry pitter, you can use an old-fashioned vegetable peeler. Hold a cherry in one hand and the peeler in the other. Insert the point of the peeler into the bottom of the cherry. Push the peeler up towards the top (where the pit is). Using your thumb on the outside of the cherry, gently press the pit against the blade of the peeler, then pull the peeler with the pit back out the bottom.

Maple Bourbon Verrine

MAKES 12 VERRINES At The Butchart Gardens, this sweet and sophisticated taste of Canadiana is served in a bourbon tumbler and garnished with a tempered chocolate leaf. Chef Travis Hansen recommends using Okanagan Spirits BRBN, a Canadian take on the American classic.

Maple mousse

9 oz white chocolate, chopped

4½ sheets gold gelatin

3½ cups whipping (33%) cream

⅓ cup + 2 Tbsp maple syrup

¼ cup maple extract

Bourbon gelée

1½ sheets gold gelatin

5¼ oz bourbon (preferably Okanagan Spirits BRBN)

2½ Tbsp sugar

1 Tbsp vanilla extract

Edible gold dust (optional)

Salted maple candied pecans

1½ cups pecan pieces

¼ cup maple syrup

¼ cup sugar

¼ tsp sea salt (preferably Maldon)

Assembly

Chocolate decorations, seasonal edible flowers, rosemary sprigs, or candied orange, for garnish (optional)

12 cookies or wafers, to serve (optional)

Maple mousse Arrange 12 small glass tumblers on a tray or baking sheet that will fit in your fridge.

Bring a small saucepan of water to a boil, then turn off the heat. Place chocolate in a heatproof bowl and set over the hot water. Stir until melted. Take care as white chocolate can burn easily.

In a small bowl, soak gelatin in lukewarm water to bloom.

In a mixer fitted with a whisk attachment, whip cream for 6 to 7 minutes, or until very soft peaks form. (If whipped too stiff, the mousse will break.)

In a small saucepan, combine maple syrup and extract and heat over medium-low until it begins to steam. Immediately remove it from the heat.

Remove gelatin from the water and squeeze out excess water. Gently lower gelatin into the hot syrup and lightly stir, until dissolved. Pour mixture into the melted chocolate and whisk vigorously.

Take a small portion of whipped cream and fold it into the chocolate maple mixture. Repeat until all ingredients are combined smoothly (do not overmix).

Evenly divide mousse among the glasses—using a jug with a pour spout helps. Transfer the tray of glasses to the fridge and chill for at least 8 hours to fully set.

Bourbon gelée In a small bowl, soak gelatin in lukewarm water to bloom.

In a small saucepan, combine bourbon, sugar and vanilla and heat over medium heat, until it begins to steam. (Be careful as the bourbon is flammable and can ignite.)

Remove bourbon mixture from heat and immerse the bloomed gelatin into it. Allow to cool slightly, then remove gelatin and squeeze out excess liquid. Stir in edible gold dust (if using) for a sparkly sheen.

Once mousse is fully set, pour the bourbon gelée over the mousse. Refrigerate for at least 8 hours, but preferably overnight, until fully set.

Salted maple candied pecans Line a baking sheet with parchment paper.

Using a non-stick frying pan, combine all ingredients and sauté over medium heat for 10 minutes, until nuts are fully coated in a dark amber caramel. Stir constantly to prevent it from burning. If needed, reduce heat.

Carefully pour the pecans onto the prepared baking sheet and set aside for 30 minutes, until very hard. Chop candied pecans to your desired size for garnish. (Candied pecans can be stored in an airtight container for up to a month.)

Assembly To serve, sprinkle a generous amount of candied pecans into each tumbler, garnish with chocolate decorations, edible flowers, rosemary sprigs, and/or candied orange (if using), and (if using) serve with a cookie (or wafer).

CANOE BREWPUB

Sam Harris

Pub culture has long been an important part of Victoria's social life. The city was home to Canada's first brew pub, boasts more than a dozen craft breweries and even has a harbour ferry pub tour. Still, it's unusual to see a celebrated fine-dining chef like Sam Harris—who has opened some of the city's most revered restaurants—in a pub kitchen.

Or is it?

"I've always loved beer pairings and the food that goes with beer," says Harris, whose first job was at a brew pub in his hometown of Ottawa. "You can go a little saltier and a little spicier. It makes for a really creative enterprise."

The location doesn't hurt, either. Canoe is located in a lofty, rambling brick building right on the city's waterfront. "It's just an amazingly beautiful building, with the harbour in front of it," Harris says. "It's such a beautiful, calming place to be."

Although the food at Canoe fits into the brew pub lexicon (as Harris puts it, "anything that goes with beer"), it has an unusual depth to it. Harris's team makes its own pickles, preserves and sausages in-house and sources from local farmers, fishers and foragers.

"We've got our own little island scene going on here. We love to focus on farm-to-table and craft cooking. We try to be accessible, but we have a lot of fun within that," he says. And besides, he adds: "I'm happy to be here at Canoe, with its craft farm food. The older I get, the more I want to be in a restaurant that my family would be comfortable in."

Roasted Cauliflower with Chimichurri, Almonds and Radish

SERVES 4 TO 6 At Canoe, the pub fare includes veggies—and why not when they are as savoury and delicious as chef Sam Harris's roasted cauliflower? The herbal flavours of the chimichurri elevate this classic side dish well above the ordinary. It can also be served as a stand-alone appetizer.

Chimichurri

3 cloves garlic, chopped

1 Tbsp chopped shallots

1½ tsp crushed red pepper

½ cup red wine vinegar

Bunch of Italian parsley, leaves only

Bunch of cilantro, leaves and stems

1 cup olive oil

1½ tsp sugar

1 tsp salt

Roasted cauliflower

1 head cauliflower, broken into large florets

¼ cup olive oil

1 Tbsp salt

¼ cup sliced almonds, toasted, for garnish

8 radishes, thinly sliced, for garnish

Chimichurri Using a food processor, combine garlic, shallots, crushed red pepper and vinegar and purée until smooth. Add parsley, cilantro, oil, sugar and salt and purée again, until well mixed. Transfer to a large bowl and set aside.

Roasted cauliflower Preheat oven to 375°F.

In a large bowl, combine cauliflower, oil and salt and toss until well coated. Transfer cauliflower to a baking sheet and roast, untouched, for 25 minutes, until tender and lightly browned.

Add hot roasted cauliflower to the bowl of chimichurri sauce and toss until coated. Transfer to a serving dish and garnish with toasted almonds and sliced radishes.

Beef, Bacon and Ricotta Meatballs with Handmade Fettuccine

SERVES 4 TO 6 Bacon and ricotta add depth and sophistication to classic meatballs, served at Canoe with a simple tomato sauce and chef Sam Harris's handmade pasta. You can use purchased pasta instead, of course.

Pasta

3 cups flour
1 tsp ground turmeric
16 egg yolks
1 Tbsp olive oil
1 Tbsp water
1 tsp salt
½ cup semolina flour, for dusting

Roasted tomato sauce

2 (796-mL) cans peeled plum tomatoes (preferably San Marzano)
1 Tbsp salt

Meatballs

½ cup milk
½ cup bread crumbs
1 lb ground beef
1 lb ground pork
¼ cup ground or finely chopped bacon
1 cup ricotta
2 Tbsp salt
1 tsp black pepper
½ tsp garlic powder
½ tsp onion powder
½ tsp crushed red pepper

Assembly

Pasta (see here)
¼ cup chopped Italian parsley
¼ cup olive oil, or to taste
1 cup grated Parmesan, or to taste

Pasta In a large bowl, combine flour and turmeric together. Create a well in the centre, then add egg yolks, oil, water and salt. Using a fork, begin incorporating flour into the centre, mixing everything together until it forms a shaggy mass. Transfer dough to a clean work surface and knead by hand for 20 minutes. Cover with plastic wrap and set aside at room temperature for at least 30 minutes.

Divide the dough into 4 equal pieces. Flatten each piece into a rectangle ½ inch thick with a floured rolling pin. Dust with semolina and cover unused portions with a cloth or plastic wrap until needed. Roll the pieces of dough through a pasta machine, starting with the thickest setting and working to the thinnest, until each sheet is ¹⁄₁₆ inch and slightly translucent. (Alternatively, roll out the dough using a rolling pin.)

Roll the sheets through the fettuccine cutter attachment or use a knife to cut into ⅜-inch-wide ribbons, dusting generously with semolina flour to prevent sticking. Form into nests until ready to use. (Cut pasta can be stored at room temperature for 4 hours or in the fridge for 2 days.)

Roasted tomato sauce Preheat oven to 375°F.

Strain tomato juice into a saucepan and cook for 15 minutes over medium heat, until reduced by half. Remove from heat.

Put strained tomatoes into a casserole dish and bake for 30 minutes, until tomatoes are lightly caramelized and slightly blackened, with concentrated flavours. Using a wooden spoon, break up tomatoes. Add to reduced tomato juice, then season with salt. Set aside.

Meatballs Preheat oven to 375°F.

In a large bowl, combine milk and bread crumbs and set aside to soak for 10 minutes. Add remaining ingredients to the bowl and mix well. With damp hands, divide mixture into 12 portions and roll into large meatballs.

Place meatballs in a casserole dish and bake, uncovered, for 25 minutes, until they start to brown.

Pour tomato sauce over meatballs. Cover with a lid or foil and bake for another 30 minutes.

Assembly Bring a large pot of salted water to a boil. Add pasta and cook for 2 to 3 minutes, or until desired doneness. Drain.

Combine with the meatballs and tomato sauce. Transfer to a serving platter and garnish with parsley, olive oil and Parmesan.

THE COURTNEY ROOM

Brian Tesolin

Entering The Courtney Room feels like stumbling across the greatest kind of best-kept secret. Its unassuming entrance at the corner of the Magnolia Hotel & Spa opens onto soaring ceilings, a gracious Old-World-meets-New World ambience and some of the finest dining in Victoria.

"We're trying to aim for that French bistro feel," says executive chef Brian Tesolin. "When the light shines downstairs, it's a magical experience." Make that a French bistro that pays homage to Italy and Japan with an exceptional pasta program and ingredients like the kampachi (amberjack) dry-aged in house. In other words, modern Pacific Northwest cuisine.

Tesolin hails from Ontario and began his career at the storied Langdon Hall in Cambridge. Since moving to Victoria in 2015, he has been smitten by all it offers—the amenities of a city, but with easy access to the outdoors. "We're 45 minutes from good wines, 40 minutes from good cheese, 20 minutes from good produce," he says. "It's like we're in cottage country, but we're not."

Although he brings specialty items like burrata and olive oil in from Italy, he sources as much as he can locally. "We have this untouched microclimate that allows us to grow products at a good price point," he says. "All the cheeses on our cheese board are from Haltwhistle up the road, and sablefish and halibut are fished in the waters just down from our house."

The Courtney Room has earned numerous awards, including an *enRoute* Top 10 Best New Restaurant nod in 2018, and is both a fine-dining destination restaurant and a favourite local hangout. Tesolin credits his former co-chef, Chris Klassen, for helping build that success. "We built this program together and that is not going to change," Tesolin says. "It's what made us what we are."

Tomato Consommé with Garden Vegetables

SERVES 8 This elegant concoction by The Courtney Room's former co-head chef Chris Klassen is the purest expression of the summery flavours we crave from tomatoes and garden vegetables. Best served chilled on a hot day as a sophisticated starter for a lunch or dinner party.

2¼ lbs tomatoes, stemmed and cut into small chunks

Bunch of basil, both leaves and stems (about 40 leaves)

2½ tsp sugar

2 tsp salt, plus extra for seasoning

1 small zucchini, thinly sliced

2 small green cucumbers, cut into ½-inch cubes

24 cherry tomatoes, halved

Juice of 1 lemon

Thinly sliced red onion (optional)

In a medium bowl, combine tomatoes, basil, sugar and salt and toss well. Cover and set aside at room temperature for 4 hours. Transfer to a blender or food processor and purée until smooth. Line a large fine-mesh sieve with cheesecloth and set over a bowl. Pour in the purée and allow it to strain in the fridge for 3 to 4 hours. Discard solids. You should have 1 litre of consommé.

In a bowl, combine zucchini, cucumbers, cherry tomatoes, and lemon juice, then season with salt. Divide among 8 bowls and pour consommé overtop. Serve chilled. Garnish with a few slices thinly sliced red onion (if using).

Tomato Consommé with Garden Vegetables, p. 59

Ricotta-Parmesan Caramelle

SERVES 4 TO 6 The Courtney Room's Brian Tesolin has invested serious time in learning how to make pasta from scratch, and this whimsical recipe shows just why it's worth making your own. Caramelle are a stuffed pasta shaped like sweets with wrappers twisted at both ends—only the wrapper is as delicious as what's inside.

Pasta dough

3½ cups Italian "00" flour or all-purpose flour, plus extra for dusting

2 tsp salt

5 eggs

4 tsp water

4 tsp olive oil

Ricotta filling

1 (454-g) tub ricotta

½ cup grated Parmesan

2 to 4 tsp truffle oil (optional)

1 to 1½ tsp salt

1 tsp black pepper

Grated zest of 2 lemons

Caramelle

Pasta Dough (see here)

Ricotta Filling (see here)

Semolina flour, for dusting

Pasta dough Using a stand mixer fitted with a hook attachment, mix flour and salt until well combined.

In a separate bowl, whisk eggs, water and oil together. Add half of the egg mixture to the dry ingredients and mix for 2 minutes, until a shaggy dough starts to form. Add the remaining half of the egg mixture and mix for another 8 to 10 minutes.

Transfer dough to a lightly floured work surface and knead for 2 to 4 minutes, until dough is smooth and pliable and springs back to shape when gently pressed. Roll dough into a ball, then wrap in plastic wrap, place in an airtight resealable bag and refrigerate for a minimum of 3 hours (and up to 12 hours).

Ricotta filling Place ricotta in a cheese-cloth-lined sieve and set aside for 1 hour to extract water. Transfer strained ricotta to a large bowl, add remaining ingredients and mix well. Season to taste. Fit a piping bag with a round tip and fill with the ricotta mixture, then refrigerate for at least 3 hours.

Caramelle Bring pasta dough to room temperature. Line a baking sheet with parchment paper and dust generously with semolina flour.

Divide the dough into 4 equal pieces. Use a floured rolling pin to flatten each piece into a ½-inch-thick rectangle. Cover any unused portion with a cloth or plastic wrap until needed. Roll the pieces of dough through a pasta machine, starting with the thickest setting and working to the second thinnest, until each sheet is ⅛-inch thick. You do not want your pasta sheet too thin as it can break once filled. (Alternatively, roll out the dough using a rolling pin.)

Place a length of pasta dough on a lightly floured work surface, making sure it is 6 inches wide. Using a pizza cutter or crimped pasta wheel, cut the sheet in half lengthwise. Then, cut each length into smaller 3- × 3½-inch rectangles. Pipe a quarter-sized dollop of filling into the centre of each rectangle. Using a pastry brush and a small bowl of water, lightly brush the pasta sheet around the filling. Fold the long side of the pasta over the filling and tuck in the end to make a tube, using your fingers to press out air and avoid creating any air pockets. Carefully twist ends as you would a candy wrapper.

Place the caramelle on the prepared baking sheet, cover and refrigerate if you aren't cooking them right away. (The caramelle can also be frozen in an airtight container for 6 months.)

Brown butter and burnt lemon sauce

Melt butter in a medium saucepan over medium-high heat, until it begins to boil. Reduce heat to medium and cook for another 5 minutes, until light brown and the fat separates. It should smell rich and nutty, like toasted hazelnuts. Strain through a fine-mesh sieve, set aside and keep warm over low heat.

Preheat broiler.

Place lemons, cut-side up, on a baking sheet and broil for 10 minutes, until very dark and nearly burnt. Set aside to cool, then juice. Strain juice and add to the brown butter, then season with salt and crushed red pepper.

Assembly Bring a large pot of salted water to a boil. (Use 2 tsp of salt per litre—the water should taste salty like the sea.) Add pasta and cook for 1½ minutes (or 3½ minutes if frozen), until al dente. Drain, reserving 1 cup pasta water.

In a large frying pan, combine butter (or oil) and a tablespoon of reserved pasta water and mix well. Add pasta and stir gently, adding more pasta water if it seems dry. Drizzle sauce overtop, then transfer to a serving platter and finish with Parmesan (or Pecorino Romano).

Brown butter and burnt lemon sauce
2 cups (4 sticks) butter
4 lemons, halved
Salt, to taste
Crushed red pepper, to taste

Assembly
Salt
2 Tbsp butter or olive oil
Grated Parmesan or
  Pecorino Romano

FRENCH PRESS
COFFEE ROASTERS
Jeremy Perkins

A couple of decades ago, Jeremy Perkins was a professional viola player back in the U.K., but tiring of the touring life and looking for a business to run. So, he says, "I decided to open a coffee shop with the French horn player." Not just any coffee shop, but a proper coffee roastery, which he ran for seventeen years.

Then Brexit came along. With his wife, Hannah, being Canadian, he decided the time was right to cross the pond. Perkins made his way to Vancouver Island and opened French Press Coffee Roasters in Qualicum Beach.

"It's a lovely community. It feels like a town in the U.K. because it has a defined town centre," Perkins says. And besides, he adds, "It's quite a stop-off for lots of people on their way to Tofino."

Qualicum Beach isn't exactly known for its edgy lifestyle or cuisine. Still, Perkins felt that it was ready for quality, hand-roasted coffee and a well-edited menu of European-style café food. "Coffee shop food doesn't have to consist solely of entry-level offerings," he says. "We should put more thought into it, especially when we are committing so much thought to the coffee we serve." The menu features sandwiches and breakfast items like shakshuka and mushroom bruschetta, as well as plenty of baked goods—carrot cake, butter tarts, lemon tarts, galettes, scones and cookies.

Of course, the coffee is the centrepiece, and it's usually organic, garden-grown coffee sourced from co-operatives and chosen with flavour foremost in mind. "We're keen on East African coffee.

At the moment we also have some from Mexico, Colombia and Peru," Perkins says. "Coffee and food have changed so much in the past twenty years, which suits the geeky part of my interests. It has to taste good first and foremost."

Shakshuka

SERVES 2 TO 4 This favourite breakfast/brunch/lunch dish at French Press Coffee Roasters is a warm hug in a bowl—fragrant with spice and hearty with tomatoes and peppers.

1 Tbsp butter

½ onion, chopped

2 to 3 cloves garlic, finely chopped

1 red bell pepper, seeded, deveined and coarsely chopped

1 Tbsp ground cumin

1 Tbsp smoked paprika

1 Tbsp ground sumac

1½ tsp ground cinnamon

¼ tsp ground cardamom

2 large vine-ripened tomatoes, coarsely chopped

1 (14-oz) can whole peeled plum tomatoes, coarsely chopped and juices reserved

¼ cup vegetable stock

1 Tbsp brown sugar

2 tsp Sriracha

4 eggs

¼ cup chopped cilantro

¼ cup crumbled feta

1 tsp grated lime zest

Salt and black pepper, to taste

Slice of your favourite bread, toasted and buttered, to serve

Melt butter in a deep, 10-inch frying pan over medium-high heat. Add onion, garlic and red pepper and sauté for 2 to 3 minutes, until aromatic. Stir in cumin, paprika, sumac, cinnamon and cardamom and sauté for another 1 to 2 minutes, until vegetables are well coated.

Add fresh tomatoes, canned tomatoes and their juices, stock, sugar and Sriracha. Bring to a boil, then reduce heat to medium-low and simmer, uncovered, for 15 to 20 minutes, until peppers are soft and cooked through.

Cover pan and bring to a vigorous boil, until it reaches a poaching temperature (about 160°F). Crack eggs into the stew, then cover pan and turn off heat. Cook on residual heat for 4 minutes, until eggs are set.

Divide the stew between bowls, using a large serving spoon to carefully transport the eggs without breaking them. Garnish with cilantro, feta and lime zest, season with salt and pepper, and enjoy with buttered toast.

Carrot Cake

MAKES 1 (9-INCH) CAKE This moist, spicy, rich and beautifully garnished treat from French Press Coffee Roasters is the best way to enjoy your veggies. The edible flowers and other garnishes are optional, but add a bright, seasonal contrast to the otherwise rustic cake.

Carrot cake
Butter, for greasing
4 cups grated carrots, loosely packed (12 oz)
1 cup flour
1 cup sugar
½ cup raisins
½ cup chopped pecans
1 tsp baking soda
1 Tbsp ground cinnamon
½ tsp ground nutmeg
½ tsp salt
3 eggs
⅔ cup vegetable oil

Garnishes (optional)
1 orange, thinly sliced
1 cup sugar
½ cup water
1 tsp coarse sea salt
Edible flowers, such as roses and marigolds

Cream cheese frosting
1 cup (2 sticks) butter, room temperature
1 cup cream cheese, room temperature
1 cup icing sugar
½ tsp salt

Carrot cake Preheat oven to 350°F. Butter a 9-inch square or round cake pan.

Using a stand mixer fitted with a paddle attachment, combine all ingredients and mix at low speed for 5 minutes, until well incorporated. Transfer batter to the prepared cake pan and bake for 45 to 55 minutes, until a toothpick inserted into the centre comes out clean. Set aside to cool.

Garnishes (optional) Preheat oven to 350°F.

Arrange orange slices in a single layer on a baking sheet and bake for 10 to 15 minutes, until just gently dried to the touch. Set aside to cool.

Line a separate baking sheet with parchment paper and set aside.

In a small saucepan, combine sugar and water and bring to a simmer over medium heat. Leave untouched for 8 to 10 minutes, until light brown. (You want to prevent the crystallization of the sugar mixture, so no stirring, but observe closely so as not to burn the caramel.)

Once the sugar turns amber, swirl the pan once to even out the colour. Immediately remove pan from the heat and pour onto the prepared baking sheet. Carefully tilt the baking sheet to thinly spread out the caramel. If you like, dip the orange slices (wholly or partway) into the caramel and set aside to cool.

Sprinkle salt overtop the remaining caramel and set aside to harden. Once solid, crack into shards.

Cream cheese frosting In a stand mixer fitted with a paddle attachment, combine all ingredients and mix on medium speed for 5 minutes, until doubled in volume. Keep at room temperature until use.

Assembly Using an offset spatula, spread cream cheese frosting over the cake. Arrange orange slices, caramel shards and edible flowers (if using) overtop.

GALIANO OCEANFRONT INN & SPA

Dean Hillier

Galiano Island is a narrow, rocky sliver of land twenty-seven kilometres long. The closest of the Gulf Islands to the mainland, it's also among the least developed—a nature lover's paradise where eagles soar overhead and orcas frolic off its shore. Sometimes guests can even see them from the Galiano Oceanfront Inn & Spa.

Little wonder then that so many people visit the island once, and then decide to stay. "I kind of fell in love with it when I got off the ferry," says Martine Paulin, the general manager of the inn. "I'd moved to B.C. from Quebec. I was going to UBC. My partner's family had a place on the island and it was like visiting a Mediterranean country. Now I've been here for twenty-seven years."

Although she's only been managing the inn since December 2019, she was previously a chef and caterer on the island, founded the Galiano Community Food Program and before that worked at some of Vancouver's top restaurants. She's excited to work collaboratively with long-time chef Dean Hillier, who's been serving up fresh seafood, local produce and the Atrevida Restaurant's famous prime rib dinners since 2004.

Paulin describes his cuisine as West Coast contemporary. "He's using local ingredients and we're in the process of replanting our kitchen garden: microgreens, herbs, edible flowers. We've got established relationships with local farmers, and I want to feature more local wines and beers on the menu, too. There are more and more amazing farms on Galiano now, and we really want to take advantage of that."

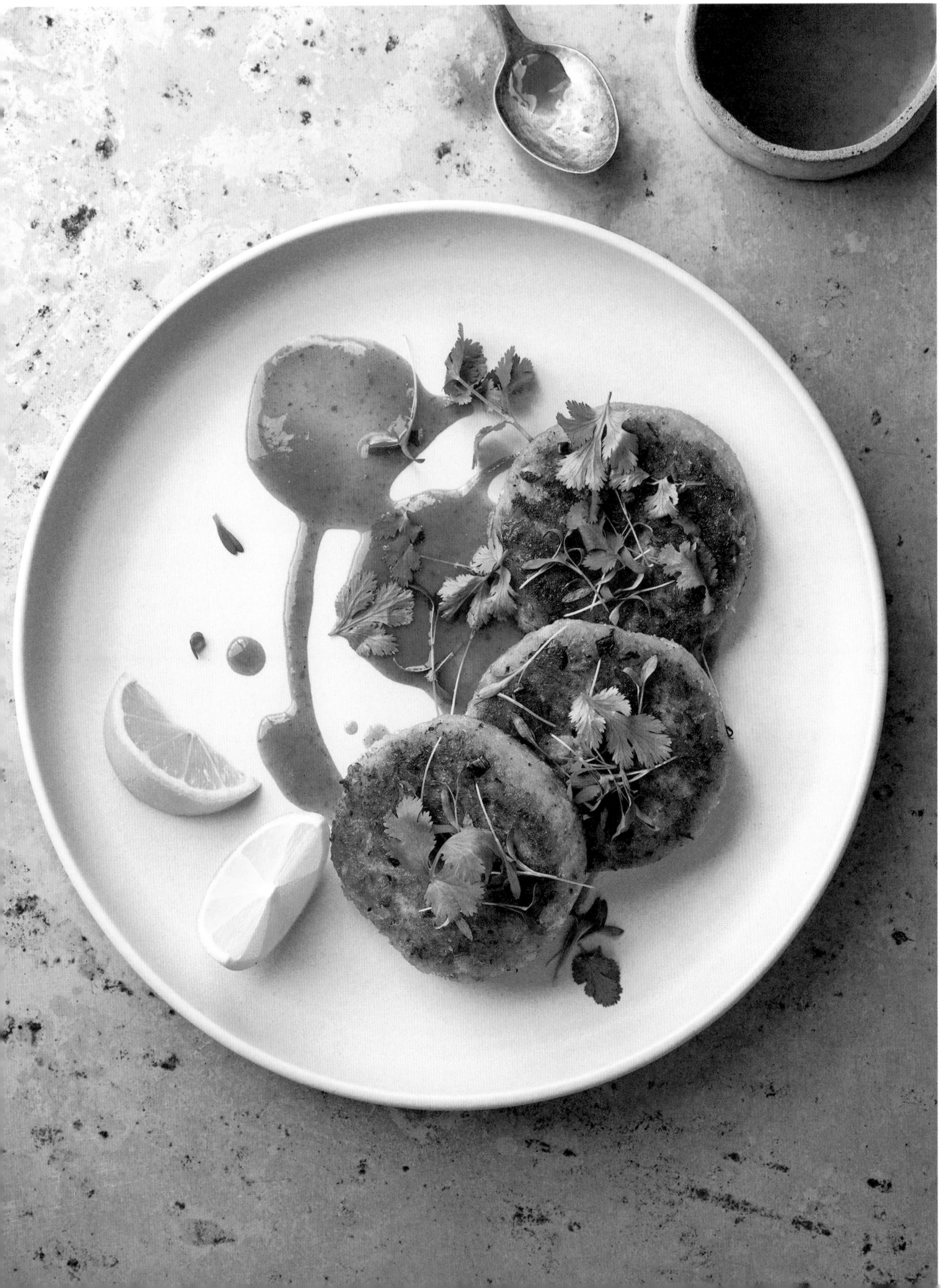

Dungeness Crab Cakes with Chipotle-Tamarind Coulis, p. 70

Dungeness Crab Cakes with Chipotle-Tamarind Coulis

SERVES 4 (AS AN APPETIZER) Sweet, tender Dungeness crab is one of the legendary ingredients of the Gulf Islands, where it is in season all year round. Galiano Inn's chef Dean Hillier forms it into crab cakes paired with a tangy, spicy tamarind sauce.

Chipotle-tamarind coulis

½ cup tamarind paste (also known as concentrate, see Note)

1 cup water

1 cup honey

1 Tbsp canned chipotle purée

¼ cup chopped cilantro

Crab cakes

¾ cup panko crumbs

¼ cup mayonnaise

3 Tbsp finely chopped red onion

3 Tbsp chopped cilantro

¼ tsp garlic purée

1 egg, beaten

Dash of Tabasco sauce

Salt and black pepper

½ lb cooked Dungeness crabmeat, well-drained and picked of shells or cartilage

2 Tbsp grapeseed or canola oil

Assembly

Chopped cilantro, for garnish

Lemon wedges, to serve (optional)

Chipotle-tamarind coulis Using a blender or food processor, combine tamarind paste and water until homogenous. Strain through a fine-mesh sieve.

In a bowl, combine the tamarind with honey, chipotle purée and cilantro. Mix well and set aside.

Note: Tamarind is a tart, aromatic ingredient popular in dishes from Southeast Asia, India, Latin America and the Middle East. It comes from a tree that produces pods filled with seeds surrounded by a sticky, fibrous and flavourful pulp, and is typically sold in one of two ways: as a block of dried pulp or in jars of paste or concentrate. To use the pulp, break the block into smaller pieces, soak them in hot water, then strain out the seeds and solids. To use the paste, either scoop it directly from the jar or, if it is too thick, dilute it with a little water.

Crab cakes In a bowl, combine panko, mayonnaise, onion, cilantro, garlic purée, egg, Tabasco and a pinch each of salt and pepper and mix well. Stir in crabmeat and refrigerate for 30 minutes to marry flavours.

Shape mixture into 8 equal-sized balls. Press down on each to form patties, 1 inch thick. (You can use a ring mould or cookie cutter to help contain the shape.)

Heat oil in a frying pan over medium-high heat. Add crab cakes, in batches to avoid overcrowding, and pan-fry for 3 minutes on each side, until golden brown.

Assembly Spread a little coulis on 4 plates, then arrange the crab cakes on top. Garnish with cilantro. If you like, serve with lemon wedges.

Rustic Artichoke and Spinach Galette

SERVES 4 At Galiano Inn, chef Dean Hillier makes a savoury rustic galette that is both vegan and gluten-free—and perfectly delicious, too.

Roast garlic
1 head garlic
1 tsp olive oil

Filling
¾ cup raw cashews
3 cloves Roasted Garlic (see here)
2 cups spinach leaves
1 cup canned artichokes, cut into ½-inch cubes
¾ cup coconut milk
¼ cup vegan cheese, such as Daiya
3 Tbsp nutritional yeast, such as Engevita
1 Tbsp olive oil
Salt and black pepper, to taste

Galette crust
3¼ cups almond meal, plus extra for dusting
6 Tbsp maple syrup
8 Tbsp cornstarch
6 Tbsp water
Pinch of salt

Assembly
½ cup spinach leaves
Microgreens or chopped Italian parsley, for garnish (optional)
Edible flowers, for garnish (optional)
Arugula salad, to serve
Side of your favourite vegetables, to serve

Roast garlic Preheat oven to 400°F.

Peel most of the skin off the head of garlic, then trim the top off the bulb (¼ inch) to expose the tops of the cloves. Drizzle with oil. Wrap in aluminum foil and bake for 40 minutes, until soft and fragrant. (Roasted garlic can be refrigerated for up to 2 weeks or frozen for up to 3 months.)

Filling Soak cashews in water at room temperature for 2 hours, until softened. (You can pour boiling water over them to speed up the process if you like.) Drain.

In a food processor, combine cashews and remaining ingredients and process until mixed but still chunky, with a rustic texture. Season with salt and pepper.

Galette crust In a large bowl, combine all ingredients and mix by hand until the dough forms a homogenous ball.

Roll out a 12-inch wide, ⅛-inch thick disk of dough by placing the chilled dough between two pieces of parchment paper or plastic wrap. (Alternatively, divide dough into 4 portions and roll out for individual galettes.)

Assembly Preheat oven to 400°F. Line a baking sheet with parchment paper.

Transfer galette disk(s) to the baking sheet. Place spinach leaves in a single layer in the centre of the crust (or 3 to 4 leaves for each individual galette). Add filling on top, leaving a ¾-inch space from the edge. Fold dough edges over to contain the filling. Bake for 25 minutes, until shell is crisp and golden brown.

Garnish the galette(s) with microgreens (or parsley) and edible flowers (if using). Serve on a bed of arugula salad with a side of vegetables.

GLO RESTAURANT + LOUNGE

Andrew Fawcett

With its unparalleled views of the Selkirk Waterway and Galloping Goose trestle, the huge patio is one of the main attractions at Glo. As owner Paul Simpson says, "Our gorgeous patio is easily the best in Victoria." But it's not the only attraction, because the drinks program and casual fine-dining menu are also major draws for this coolly contemporary space.

Chef Andrew Fawcett, who also helped Simpson open Boom + Batten (page 34) and Med Grill, brings a passion for local ingredients and global flavours to a menu that has something for everyone, from Sunday brunch to late-night happy hour.

"I love all types of food so it's hard to pin my favourite flavours," Fawcett says. "We do ahi tuna bowls and pastas, but we also do great flatbreads. And we have an amazing steak program."

Glo also has a large list of share plates, casual entrées, burgers and other specialties. Guest favourites include the Shanghai lettuce wraps, tuna tataki, Buddha bowl and the very popular appetizer list. Making a large majority of their options entirely in-house, Fawcett sources locally as much as possible. "We work hard to source amazing products and offer them at a great value to our customers daily."

With among the largest happy-hour and late-night menus in the city, Glo's Selkirk waterfront location and close proximity to downtown makes it a hot spot for locals and tourists day and night.

Tan Tan City Salad

SERVES 4 This bright salad by Glo Restaurant's Andrew Fawcett is bursting with healthy ingredients and lively fusion flavours.

Honey-lime dressing

1¼ cups grapeseed oil

¼ cup lime juice

3 Tbsp apple cider vinegar

3 Tbsp honey

1 egg yolk

Grated zest and juice of 1 lime

Salt, to taste

Salad

4 boneless, skinless
  chicken breasts

½ to ¾ cup Cajun spice blend

4 cups local mixed greens

¾ cup Honey-Lime Dressing
  (see here)

2 oranges, skin and pith
  removed, segmented

1 ripe avocado, thinly sliced

½ cup pitted dried dates

½ cup sliced or slivered
  almonds, toasted

4 oz goat cheese, crumbled

8 mint leaves

1 lime, cut into wedges

Honey-lime dressing Use a blender or food processor to combine all ingredients and blend until silky smooth. Pour into a Mason jar and refrigerate until needed. Makes 1¾ cups. (Dressing can be stored in the fridge for up to 2 weeks.)

Salad Preheat grill over high heat.

Generously season chicken with the Cajun spice blend.

Place chicken on grill and cook for 4 to 5 minutes. Turn, then cook for another 4 to 5 minutes, until cooked through. Transfer chicken to a plate and let rest for 3 to 5 minutes. Slice.

Toss mixed greens with a little of the honey-lime dressing and divide among 4 plates. Top with oranges, avocado slices, dates, almonds, goat cheese and mint. Drizzle the rest of the dressing overtop. Top with grilled chicken breast and serve with lime wedges.

Spicy Kung Pao Tofu Bowl

SERVES 4 The Asian flavours chef Andrew Fawcett loves so much come through vibrantly in this vegan noodle bowl from Glo Restaurant.

Spicy Szechuan sauce

1 tsp sesame oil

¼ cup finely chopped white onion

1 clove garlic, finely chopped

2 Tbsp finely chopped ginger

1 small green onion, thinly sliced

½ cinnamon stick

1 pod star anise

2 Tbsp brown sugar

¼ tsp crushed red pepper

¾ cup soy sauce

⅓ cup water + 1 Tbsp (divided)

2 tsp cornstarch

1 cup Thai sweet chili sauce

1 Tbsp sesame seeds

Kung pao

1 (14-oz) bag Chinese steam fried noodles, such as Farkay noodles

2 Tbsp vegetable oil

1 carrot, shaved

1 red onion, thinly sliced

2 small heads broccoli, cut into florets

8 white mushrooms, sliced

1 cup snap peas (6 oz)

1 (350-g) package firm organic tofu, cubed

1½ cups Spicy Szechuan Sauce (see here)

2 cups bean sprouts

¾ cup cashews, chopped

12 sprigs cilantro, chopped

1 lime, cut into wedges

Spicy Szechuan sauce Heat oil in a medium saucepan over medium heat. Add white onions and sauté for 5 to 7 minutes, until they have softened. Add garlic and ginger and cook for another 2 minutes. Add green onions, cinnamon, star anise, brown sugar and crushed red pepper. Pour in soy sauce and ⅓ cup water. Bring to a boil, then reduce heat to medium-low and simmer for 30 minutes. Strain sauce through a fine-mesh sieve into another saucepan and discard the solids.

Heat sauce over medium heat. In a small bowl, mix cornstarch and 1 table-spoon water to create a slurry. Add slurry to pan and simmer 2 minutes, until sauce has thickened. Stir in sweet chili sauce and sesame seeds. Set aside. (Sauce can be stored in the fridge for up to 30 days.)

Kung pao Cook noodles according to package instructions, then set aside to cool.

Heat oil in a large frying pan over medium heat. Add carrot, red onions, broccoli, mushrooms, snap peas and tofu. Sauté for 3 to 4 minutes, until vegetables have slightly softened.

Pour in sauce and mix well. Add noodles and cook for 2 minutes, until noodles are well coated and heated through.

Divide among 4 bowls, then top with bean sprouts, cashews, cilantro and lime wedges.

HARDY BUOYS SMOKED FISH

Carol Dirom and Kellie Dukes

Bruce and Carol Dirom met when they were teenagers in the Cowichan Valley and moved to remote Port Hardy when he got a job with BC Hydro. The plan was to stay two years. Then they fell in love with the pristine wilderness, family-friendly lifestyle and especially the fishing. But if they were to stay, they needed another source of income. So they turned to Bruce's hobby.

"Bruce used to clean his fish in a bathtub and he used to smoke them in an old fridge in the backyard," Carol says. "He loves fishing and the rules were a lot different back then. People could smoke and can as much fish as they wanted." When new limits were imposed, sport fishermen needed someone to preserve their fish for them. Enter the Diroms.

In 1994, they opened Hardy Buoys Smoked Fish with one additional employee and a 3,000-square-foot space. Today, they employ sixty-five people year-round and work out of a 50,000-square-foot automated facility—preparing fish for wholesale, food service, and recreational and commercial fishermen.

"We're best known for hot-smoked salmon, especially the candied salmon," Carol says, noting that ninety-five percent of their business is salmon, much of it under private labels and Ocean Wise approved. The fish is dry-brined, then smoked over alder chips. "We have smoke masters who are constantly checking and turning racks. It's artisan and small batch."

For these recipes, Carol turned to her friend Kellie Dukes, who has a weekly Facebook cooking show called *Dukes Dining* and makes a sushi pizza the Diroms especially love. "The pizza is so good I've had to fight my husband for it," Carol says. For her part, Dukes is a huge fan of Hardy Buoys, and says, "I would never go anywhere else for my smoked salmon."

Smoked Salmon–Goat Cheese Tartlets

MAKES 12 TARTLETS These pretty little tarts created by Kellie Dukes for Hardy Buoys Smoked Fish are a tempting canapé for a social gathering, or a lovely indulgence for yourself.

2 sheets puff pastry (frozen and thawed is fine)

1½ cups huckleberries, plus 36 for garnish (see Note)

1 Tbsp sugar

¼ cup water

½ tsp lime juice

1 green onion, thinly sliced diagonally (divided)

10 oz soft, unripened goat cheese

¼ cup plain Greek yogurt

12 Hardy Buoys Smoked Fish's Smoked Salmon Nuggets

Preheat oven to 350°F. If it's not pre-rolled, roll out the puff pastry to 10 × 15 inches, ¼ inch thick.

Cut each sheet of puff pastry into 6 (5-inch) squares. Place each square into alternate cups of two regular-sized muffin pans so that no puff pastry squares are next to each other. Do not tuck in corners of squares. Bake for 30 to 35 minutes, until golden brown.

The puff pastry shells will have puffed closed. Using the back of a spoon, press down the centres to create a hole for the filling without piercing the pastry. Carefully transfer shells to a wire rack and set aside to cool completely.

Combine the 1½ cups berries with sugar and water in a small saucepan and bring to a simmer over medium heat. Reduce heat to low, then use the back of a wooden spoon to break up the huckleberries. Cook, stirring occasionally, for 25 minutes, until thickened. Do not let the sauce burn.

Remove sauce from heat and stir in lime juice. Strain through a fine-mesh sieve into a bowl. Discard solids.

Meanwhile, reserve 12 slices of green onion for garnish. In a bowl, cream together goat cheese, yogurt and remaining green onions until smooth.

Spoon 2 tablespoons of the cheese mixture into the centre of each puff pastry tartlet shell. Top with a smoked salmon nugget and press slightly into the goat cheese to secure it in place. Transfer tartlets to a serving plate. Arrange 3 huckleberries together at one corner of each salmon nugget. Next to the huckleberries, place a slice of the green onion to make it "holly-like" in appearance. Drizzle ½ tsp of huckleberry sauce overtop each tartlet and serve.

Note: If you are unable to find huckleberries, you can use blueberries, blackberries, raspberries or cranberries. When using these larger berries, you only need one berry per tart as a garnish, so 12 berries in total.

Smoked Salmon Sushi Pizza

MAKES 2 (5-INCH) PIZZAS Kellie Dukes created this casual riff on sushi for Hardy Buoys, using salmon that is brined, smoked and "candied" using a secret sauce until it becomes smoky-sweet and tender. Be sure to use sushi rice, a short-grained variety that becomes soft and sticky when cooked.

1½ cups water

1 cup sushi rice

2 Tbsp rice vinegar

1 tsp sugar

1 tsp wasabi paste

2 tsp Japanese mayonnaise

2 sheets nori, each cut into a 5-inch circle

1 avocado, thinly sliced

2 Tbsp finely diced carrots

4-inch piece English cucumber, seeded and cut into matchsticks

18 large flakes of smoked salmon, preferably belly meat (see Note)

1 green onion, thinly sliced diagonally

¼ to ½ cup flying fish roe (tobiko)

Sriracha (optional)

2 tsp toasted sesame seeds

Bring water to a boil over high heat in a small saucepan. Stir in rice. Reduce heat to low, then cover and simmer for 20 minutes, until rice is cooked through. Remove from heat and set aside, covered, for 10 minutes. Stir in vinegar and sugar, then fluff with a fork. Set aside to cool completely.

Dampen hands with water. Place rice on a cutting board and make 2 round rice "pizza" bases, 5 inches in diameter and ¾ inch thick. Press the rice lightly so it sticks together. Place on 2 plates.

Gently spread wasabi paste evenly over the bases. Top each with mayonnaise and a nori sheet. Arrange avocado, carrots and cucumbers on top, covering edge to edge. Arrange salmon flakes in a star shape going out from the centre to the edge.

Garnish with small dollops of roe and green onion slices between the flakes. Add a dot of Sriracha atop each flake (if using). Sprinkle with toasted sesame seeds and serve.

Note: Although you can use any type of smoked salmon for this dish, Carol Dirom recommends the Hardy Buoys Atlantic Salmon Candy, which is especially tender and a little bit sweet.

HATTIE'S FARM TO TABLE

Ljubek Dehlic and Brigitte Guerin

The summer of 2020 was not a great time for anyone in the restaurant business. A global pandemic had shut everyone down in March, and restaurateurs were slowly reopening—many with limited hours, many serving only takeout. But not Duncan's Andrea Flemming. "The break, the forced shutdown, had a silver lining," she says. "I had a beautiful summer with my daughter, time I have not had with her since she was born." And it gave Flemming time to reinvent her business.

She still loved her "beautiful boutique restaurant" that was "very community-focused and local farm-focused," but it was time for a new name, a new vision and a new culinary team for what had formerly been called Hudson's on First.

Flemming hired a talented husband-and-wife chef team: Ljubek Dehlic and Brigitte Guerin, he to take on savoury and she patisserie. They had worked in some of Vancouver's top restaurants—Guerin also worked at Michelin-starred restaurants back home in her native France—and had friends and former employers in common with Flemming, as well as a passion for local products and sustainable practices. "This was a big move for all of us," Flemming says.

Together they've been discovering exciting local products like the tisanes from Westholme Tea Company and the passionfruit grown on Salt Spring Island. "Our menu is very tight and very focused," Flemming says. "We have unique ingredients that are handled in a very complementary way."

As for that restaurant name, she changed it to Hattie's Farm to Table, named for the original builder of the 1906 heritage house, a shipwright named Daniel Hattie. Bringing past and present together, deliciously.

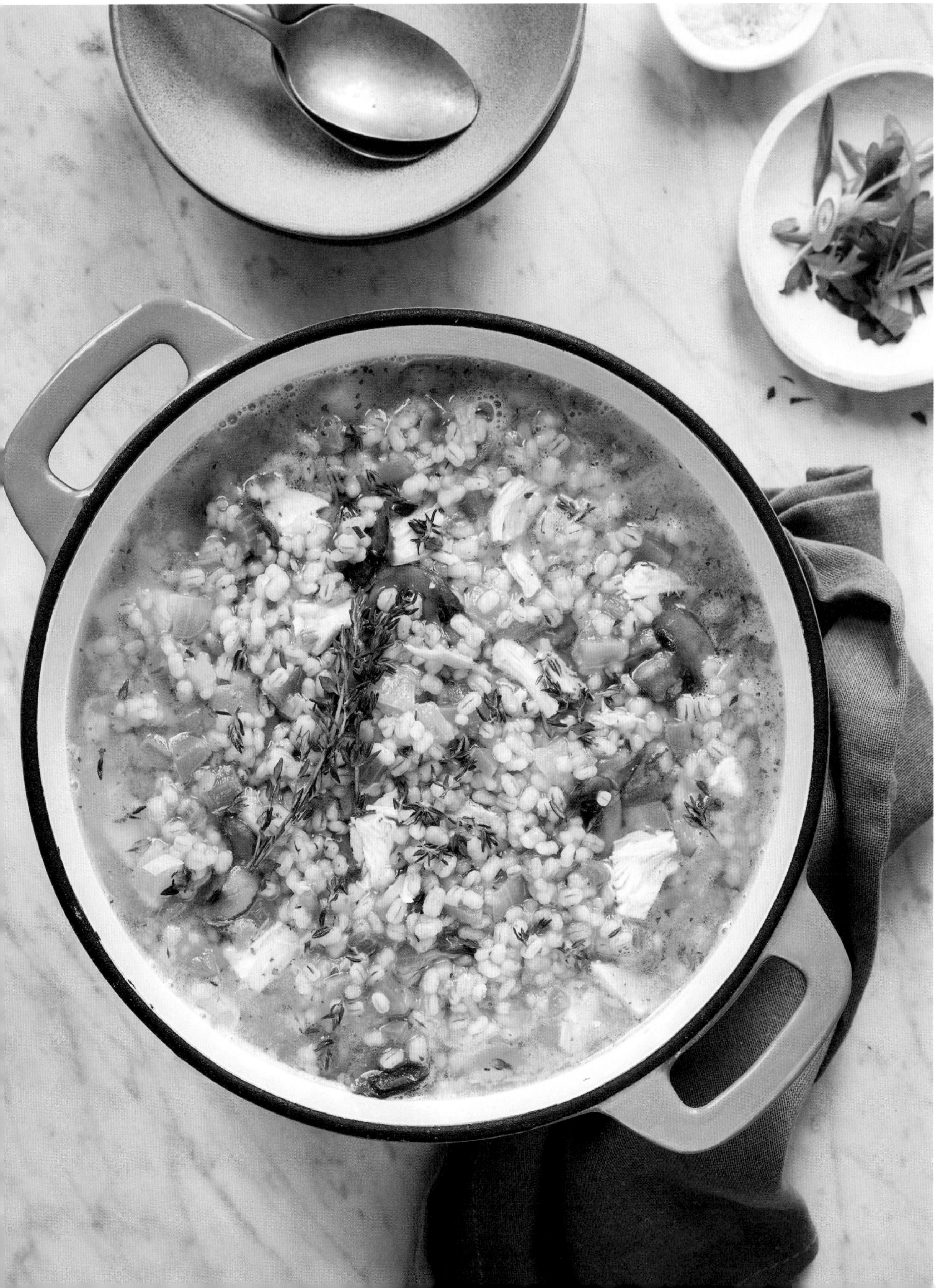

Chicken Barley Soup, p. 82

Chicken Barley Soup

SERVES 8 TO 10 With Hattie's Farm to Table being located on the edge of the Cowichan Valley, chef Ljubek Dehlic has an abundance of farm-fresh ingredients to use in hearty dishes such as this rib-sticking soup. Roasting the chicken bones first adds a rich flavour and golden colour.

Chicken stock

3½ lbs chicken bones

5 quarts water

1 large onion, quartered

1 large leek, white and light green parts only, halved lengthwise

2 stalks celery, cut into 2-inch pieces

1 large carrot, cut into 1-inch pieces

1 head garlic

Pinch of salt

6 sprigs thyme

Sprig of rosemary

1 Tbsp whole black peppercorns

4 bay leaves

Chicken barley soup

4 bone-in, skin-on chicken thighs or leftover roast chicken meat

Salt and black pepper

2 to 3 Tbsp vegetable oil

12 cremini mushrooms, sliced

3 stalks celery, finely chopped

1 onion, finely chopped

1 carrot, finely chopped

1 leek, white and light green parts only, halved lengthwise and sliced

2 cloves garlic, chopped

1 Tbsp thyme leaves

1 tsp chopped rosemary

Pinch of crushed red pepper

4 bay leaves

Chicken Stock (see here)

1¾ cups pearl barley (12 oz)

¼ cup chopped Italian parsley

2 green onions, chopped

Red wine vinegar, to taste

Chicken stock Preheat oven to 400°F.

Place chicken bones in a roasting pan and roast for 30 to 40 minutes, stirring occasionally, until bones are evenly browned and dark golden. Reserve pan with any drippings. Transfer bones to a stockpot, add water, and bring to a boil over medium-high heat. As stock reaches a near boil, skim any impurities from the surface and discard. Do not allow your stock to boil fully or else the fat will emulsify into the stock and make it cloudy.

Place the vegetables in the roasting pan with the drippings and sprinkle with a pinch of salt. Roast for 20 minutes.

Add vegetables to the stock. If desired, deglaze the roasting pan with ½ cup water and add to stock, along with the herbs and spices. Simmer over low heat for 6 hours. Strain through a fine-mesh sieve and reserve. Discard solids.

Chicken barley soup Preheat oven to 400°F.

Season uncooked chicken with salt and pepper. Heat a large ovenproof frying pan over medium-high heat, then add the thighs, skin-side down, and sear until golden. Turn thighs over, place pan in oven and roast for 20 minutes, until cooked through. Remove from oven and allow to cool.

Meanwhile, add 2 tablespoons oil to a stockpot over medium-high heat, then cook the mushrooms until caramelized. Reduce temperature to medium-low, add the remaining vegetables and the thyme, rosemary, crushed red pepper and bay leaves. Season with a pinch of salt and pepper. Sweat for 10 minutes, until tender.

Add stock and bring to a simmer. Add barley and simmer for 25 minutes on medium-low heat, until barley is tender.

Remove chicken meat from bones and cut (with skin on) into bite-sized pieces. Add chicken to the pot and cook for 2 to 3 minutes, until heated through. Stir in parsley and green onions, then season to taste with salt and pepper. Add a splash of vinegar and serve.

Note: The stock can be made up to three days beforehand—keep refrigerated until ready to use. It can also be stored in the freezer for up to three months.

Blossom Tea Panna Cotta with Pears and Hazelnuts

SERVES 5 One of the most exciting producers in the Cowichan Valley is Westholme Tea Company, Canada's only organic commercial tea grower. They also import teas, like the one chef Brigitte Guerin uses in this panna cotta—it's a blend of Chinese jasmine tea and white peony tea with a lovely floral bouquet. If you can't find it, use any fragrant tea you like.

Stewed pears

4 pears, peeled, cored and cut into a ¼-inch dice

3 Tbsp sugar

2½ Tbsp water

⅛ tsp agar agar

Panna cotta

2 cups whipping (33%) cream (divided)

¼ cup sugar

1½ Tbsp Westholme Tea Company Blossom blend tea or tea leaves of your choice

2½ sheets gelatin or 1½ tsp powdered gelatin

Assembly

½ cup blanched hazelnuts

1 ripe pear, peeled, cored and thinly sliced

Mint leaves

Stewed pears Combine pears, sugar and water in a medium saucepan over low heat. Cook for 5 to 10 minutes until tender. Add agar agar and stir for a minute.

Divide the cooked pears between 5 ramekins or bowls and level out. Refrigerate to cool and set.

Panna cotta In a medium saucepan, combine 1 cup cream with sugar and tea leaves and bring to a boil over medium heat. Turn heat to low and simmer for 5 minutes. Strain and discard tea leaves, then hold tea-infused cream on low heat.

In a small bowl, soak gelatin in lukewarm water for 5 minutes, until soft. Remove gelatin from the water and squeeze out excess water. Add it to the tea cream and whisk until fully dissolved.

(If you are using powdered gelatin, just whisk it into the warm tea cream.) Whisk in the remaining 1 cup of cream.

Divide the tea cream between the ramekins (or bowls) and refrigerate for at least 2 hours to set.

Assembly Preheat oven to 350°F. Line a baking sheet with parchment paper.

Place hazelnuts on the prepared baking sheet and toast for 8 to 10 minutes, until golden and fragrant. Set aside to cool. Fold parchment overtop of your hazelnuts and use the bottom of a saucepan or a rolling pin to crush them.

Arrange slices of pear overtop the panna cotta, sprinkle with crushed hazelnuts and garnish with mint leaves.

HEARTWOOD KITCHEN
FOOD OUTFITTER

Ian Riddick

After a lifetime of overseeing hotel kitchens, when Ian Riddick opened his own place in Ucluelet in 2018 he "didn't want to pigeonhole it too much." And so Heartwood is a restaurant, but also a catering company, an outfitter, a cooking school, a place for grab-and-go lunches and, once in a while, a pop-up Chinese takeout joint. "I wanted to get back to cooking," Riddick says. "This gave me a chance to do what I want."

Riddick started cooking when he was just fifteen, back in Toronto, and spent decades working mostly for Delta Hotels, moving ever further west. Eventually he ended up in Tofino, at Long Beach Lodge Resort, and fell in love with the wild west coast, its incredible ingredients and its "amazing culture of chefs." As he says, "I loved the climate. Summers are amazing. My priorities were shifting to a better lifestyle, too."

Then he learned that a heritage building down the road in Ucluelet was for sale, and Heartwood was born. "It was a restaurant before we bought it. We opened the kitchen because I love to entertain and be part of the experience," he says. But he also loves catering weddings and doing "old-school *garde-manger* work." He loves the spontaneity of changing his menu on the fly if someone drops off twenty pounds of chuck flats or a bucket of chanterelles. And he loves inviting his neighbours in to be guest chefs for a night while he assists them.

"We have this improvisational spirit so we can adapt to whatever we need to do at the time," Riddick says. "In a tricky market like this, I needed to do more things, something that would allow me to change as my years go on. That's the true spirit of Heartwood Kitchen."

Chanterelle Mushroom Pâté

MAKES 3 CUPS Come fall, the forests around Ucluelet are filled with wild mushrooms, especially tender golden chanterelles. They feature twice in this recipe from chef Ian Riddick—first as a vegetarian pâté, then as a quick-pickled garnish to add a bright, tangy note. Served with crackers or bread, this pâté makes for a terrific appetizer.

Pâté

2 Tbsp olive oil

2 shallots, thinly sliced

4 cups packed chanterelle mushrooms, cleaned (See Note)

½ cup toasted hazelnuts, peeled and roughly chopped

1 cup white wine

1½ cups whipping (33%) cream

1 to 2 Tbsp salt, or to taste

1 tsp black pepper, or to taste

1 Tbsp thyme leaves, chopped

Pickled chanterelles

1 cup water

1 cup white vinegar

½ cup sugar

1 tsp fennel seeds

1 tsp mustard seeds

1 tsp salt

1 bay leaf

1 small onion, thinly sliced

4 cups packed chanterelle mushrooms, cleaned (See Note)

Assembly

Baguette, crostini, flatbread or crackers, to serve

Pâté Heat oil in a saucepan over medium heat. Add shallots and sauté for 2 minutes, until soft and translucent, but not browned.

Add chanterelles and sauté for 8 to 10 minutes to release water. Add hazelnuts and wine and cook for another 10 minutes, until liquid has reduced and mixture begins to dry in pan. Keep a close eye at this stage.

Add cream and cook for another 10 minutes, until mixture thickens. Add salt and pepper, then stir in thyme.

Transfer mixture to a food processer fitted with a blade attachment and process to your desired consistency. (It can be either very smooth or textured.) Transfer into individual ramekins or a large container and cover. (It can be stored in the fridge for up to 7 days.)

Pickled chanterelles In a saucepan, combine all ingredients, except for the mushrooms. Bring to a simmer and cook for 2 minutes.

Add mushrooms to the pickling liquid and simmer for 15 minutes over medium-low heat. The mushrooms will tighten up as they absorb the pickling liquid. Remove from heat and set aside to cool to room temperature. (Pickled mushrooms can be stored in an airtight container in the fridge for up to 2 weeks.)

Note: This is a quick fridge pickle, not a recipe for canning. Quick pickles are easier to make than regular or fermented pickles—simply pour a solution of vinegar, water, salt and sometimes sugar and spices over fresh vegetables, and they're ready to eat within a few hours. However, unlike canning, which creates an environment where micro-organisms cannot grow, quick pickling is a short-term preservation process. Quick pickles must be refrigerated and consumed within a few weeks, and no more than 2 weeks for onions, garlic or mushrooms, which are especially susceptible to food-borne illnesses.

Assembly Arrange ramekins of pâté on plates or a platter. (Alternatively, shape pâté into quenelles and place directly on the plates.) Garnish with chanterelle pickles and serve cold with baguette, crostini, flatbread or crackers.

Note: Chanterelles can be substituted with commercially grown mushrooms or rehydrated dried mushrooms.

Seared Scallops with Vancouver Island Root Succotash and Corn Purée

SERVES 4 The sweet, earthy flavours of chef Ian Riddick's succotash and corn purée are the perfect foil for the richness of the seared scallops.

Corn purée

1 Tbsp butter

1 shallot, thinly sliced

2 cups fresh or frozen corn

1 cup skim or 2% milk

1 tsp salt, or to taste

Succotash

1 small butternut squash, peeled and cut into ½-inch cubes (2 cups)

1 large celeriac (celery root), peeled and cut into ½-inch cubes (2 cups)

2 Tbsp canola oil

Salt and black pepper, to taste

3 slices bacon, chopped

1 cup whipping (33%) cream

1 cup fresh or frozen corn

Scallops

½ cup canola oil, plus extra if needed

20 large (10/20 size) fresh scallops, muscle removed

Salt and black pepper, to taste

Seasonal greens, like basil and sorrel leaves, to serve (optional)

Corn purée Melt butter in a saucepan over medium heat. Add shallots and cook for 3 to 5 minutes, until shallots are softened and translucent. Add corn and milk, bring to a simmer and cook for 5 to 6 minutes. Season with salt.

Using an immersion blender, purée until smooth. Add a little more salt if needed. Keep warm.

Succotash Preheat oven to 375°F. Line a baking sheet with parchment paper.

In a large bowl, combine squash, celeriac and oil and toss. Season lightly with salt and pepper. Place on the prepared baking sheet and roast for 15 minutes, until cooked through. Set aside.

In a non-stick frying pan over medium-high heat, sauté bacon for 5 minutes, until fat has rendered and bacon begins to crisp. Drain excess bacon fat, leaving 2 tablespoons (enough to just coat the root vegetables).

Return pan to stove, reduce to medium heat and add squash, celeriac and whipping cream. Cook for another 3 to 5 minutes, until cream has reduced by half. Stir in corn, then season with salt and pepper. Keep warm.

Scallops Heat oil to a depth of ¼ inch in a large frying pan over medium-high heat. Pat scallops dry and season with salt and pepper, then add to the pan in batches (to avoid overcrowding). Sear scallops for 1 to 1½ minutes, until a golden brown crust forms. Flip scallop over and sear for another 1 to 1½ minutes, until browned and cooked medium-rare to medium. Transfer to a paper towel–lined plate to rest. Repeat with remaining scallops and top up with more oil, if necessary.

Assembly Divide the hot corn purée among 4 plates and spread out using the back of a spoon. Add succotash to the centre of each plate, then arrange 5 scallops on top. Garnish with season greens, (if using). Serve immediately.

IL FALCONE

Andrey Durbach

It was the opportunity to "be the master of my fate" that brought Andrey Durbach to the Comox Valley after owning and operating some of Vancouver's most exciting restaurants. For the first time, he could own the building, too—in this case, a charming ochre heritage house surrounded by quince, fig and cherry trees just steps from Courtenay's commercial strip.

He trained at the Culinary Institute of America in New York and cooked at just about every Vancouver restaurant of note in the 1990s, including Bishop's, Il Giardino and Bacchus. And then he opened, in relatively short order, Étoile, Parkside, La Buca, Pied à Terre, Cafeteria and Sardine Can, at one point running four restaurants with four different types of cuisine, all at the same time. "It was a good challenge and a great experience, but I had reached a point in my life where I wished to focus my energies on one truly excellent establishment, without a landlord," he says.

Moving to the Island allowed him to indulge in his love of ingredient-driven Italian food. "My plan for Il Falcone was to combine the best local and imported ingredients together," he says. Dishes tend to be fairly traditional—Caprese salad, osso buco (page 89), bistecca alla Fiorentina, panna cotta—prepared with finesse and fine ingredients.

"Come out here and you have so many producers supplying a much smaller marketplace. And I have first crack at everything," he says gleefully. "I can buy spot prawns off the boat in Comox Harbour and there are five or six people in the valley growing great heirloom tomatoes. Since prices can stay reasonable, I can put more money into the wine." We'll drink to that.

Osso Buco Milanese

SERVES 4 Il Falcone chef-owner Andrey Durbach says: "Please note this is an expensive, luxurious braised dish that relies on top-quality meat and careful, attentive cooking. Be sure to use hind shanks of veal, not the fore shanks. (And don't be tempted because they are considerably cheaper!) This dish cannot be rushed. If you don't have time to make it, don't make it."

Osso buco

4 (14-oz) centre-cut pieces veal hind shanks, full marrow bones
Salt and black pepper, to taste
Flour, for dusting
¼ cup olive oil, plus extra if needed
1 carrot, finely chopped
1 stalk celery, finely chopped
1 onion, finely chopped
3 cloves garlic, finely chopped
4 basil leaves, finely chopped
2 sage leaves, finely chopped
1 bay leaf
Small sprig of rosemary, finely chopped
½ tsp fennel seeds
1½ to 2 cups chicken or beef stock, plus extra if needed
1½ cups tomato passata
1½ cups dry white wine

Risotto Milanese

2 Tbsp olive oil
¼ cup (½ stick) butter (divided)
½ onion, finely chopped
1 cup carnaroli rice (do not use arborio)
Salt and black pepper, to taste
1¼ tsp saffron
Grated zest of ½ lemon
1½ cups chicken stock
½ cup dry white wine
6 Tbsp grated Parmesan or Grana Padano

Gremolata (optional)

½ cup finely chopped Italian parsley
Grated zest of 2 lemons
1 clove garlic, grated

Osso buco Preheat oven to 300°F.

Pat veal shanks dry with a paper towel and generously season all over with salt and black pepper. Dust both sides of the veal shanks with flour, tapping off any excess.

Heat oil in a large Dutch oven over medium-high heat. (Add more oil if necessary to generously coat the bottom.) Add 2 veal shanks to the pan and fry for 5 to 10 minutes, until browned. Turn over and fry for another 5 to 10 minutes, until browned. Transfer to a plate and set aside along with any accumulated juices. Repeat with remaining shanks.

Return Dutch oven to heat, adding more oil if necessary. Add carrots, celery, onions, garlic, basil, sage, bay leaf, rosemary and fennel seeds. Reduce heat to medium and cook for 3 to 5 minutes, until onions are softened and translucent.

Add veal shanks back to the pan in a single layer and cover with stock, passata and wine. Bring to a boil, then cover and place in the oven. Braise for 3 to 4 hours, basting every 45 minutes. There needs to be a sufficient amount of liquid to baste the meat, while covering at least three-quarters of the shanks. If needed, top up with more stock or water.

Uncover and cook for another 15 minutes. Remove from oven and set aside, covered, for at least 15 to 20 minutes.

Risotto Milanese Preheat oven to 475°F.

Heat oil and 2 tablespoons butter in a deep ovenproof saucepan over medium heat. Add onions and sauté for 1 to 2 minutes. Do not brown. Stir in rice and mix well until coated. Season with salt and pepper, then add saffron and lemon zest. Stir for another 30 seconds.

Add stock and wine and bring to a boil, stirring constantly. Cover and bake for 11 minutes.

Remove risotto from oven and set aside, covered, for another 2 minutes. Stir in the remaining 2 tablespoons of butter and the cheese. If the rice is undercooked or too dry, you can adjust the consistency by returning the pan to the stovetop, adding a little water and cooking over medium-low heat for another 3 to 5 minutes, stirring vigorously with a wooden spoon.

Gremolata (optional) In a small bowl, combine all ingredients and mix well.

Assembly Spoon risotto onto 4 plates, arrange osso buco on top and sprinkle with a generous amount of gremolata (if using). And since we're doing it right, open that bottle of Barolo you've always wanted to try and drink it alongside.

Note: Risotto Milanese, or saffron risotto, is an essential accompaniment to Osso Buco Milanese. "These two are always served together. Always. You can eat osso buco without saffron risotto, but you're not eating Osso Buco Milanese unless you're also eating Risotto Milanese."

Caramel Panna Cotta

SERVES 8 At Il Falcone, chef-owner Andrey Durbach adds salted caramel sauce and crunchy hazelnut praline to classic panna cotta for a swoonily rich and sweet dessert.

Panna cotta

1 (300-mL) can condensed milk
4 cups whipping (33%) cream
¼ cup brandy
½ tsp salt
6 sheets gelatin

Salted caramel sauce

1 cup sugar
½ cup water
¼ cup (½ stick) butter
¾ cup whipping (33%) cream
1 tsp fine sea salt

Hazelnut praline

Non-stick cooking spray
2 cups sugar
½ cup (1 stick) butter
½ cup water
⅓ cup light corn syrup
½ tsp baking soda
2 cups toasted hazelnuts or other favourite nut

Assembly

Crème fraîche or whipped cream, to serve

Panna cotta Peel label off condensed milk can. Place unopened can on its side in a large saucepan, then add enough water to cover the can by 2 inches. Bring to a boil, then reduce to a lively simmer and cook for 2 hours, making sure the can is always covered in water. Top up with more hot water if necessary.

Using tongs, remove the can of condensed milk from the pan and run under cold running water until cool enough to handle. Open. You will have a soft, rich, sweet, deep golden-brown caramel known as dulce de leche.

In a large saucepan, combine cream, brandy and salt and bring to a near boil. Reduce heat to medium-low and gently simmer. Pour in caramel and whisk until smooth.

In a small bowl, soak gelatin in lukewarm water for 3 to 4 minutes, until softened. Remove gelatin and squeeze out excess water. Whisk gelatin into the caramel mixture until combined.

Pour into a large serving dish or into 8 ramekins or glasses, then chill for at least 4 hours until set.

Salted caramel sauce Bring sugar and water to a boil in a medium saucepan. Add butter, reduce heat to medium, and cook for 3 to 4 minutes, until a deep golden amber in colour.

Working quickly and carefully, remove pan from heat and pour in cream. Vigorously whisk the bubbling caramel sauce until it begins to subside, then add salt. Reduce heat to low and cook for another minute, until silky smooth. Set aside to cool.

Hazelnut praline Line a baking sheet with parchment paper. Generously spray paper with cooking spray.

Attach a candy thermometer to a tall-sided, heavy-bottomed saucepan. Combine sugar, butter, water and corn syrup and cook over medium-high heat until temperature reads 300°F (hard-crack stage).

Remove from heat, then add baking soda, which will cause mixture to bubble up. Quickly stir in hazelnuts, then immediately pour mixture onto the prepared baking sheet and spread with a silicone spatula. Mixture should lie as flat as possible. This is a very sticky operation so you'll need to work quickly and safely. Oven mitts are perhaps a good idea for the less confident. Set aside to cool and harden.

Break up and pulse in a food processor to make praline. (Or just break up instead and eat as brittle.)

Assembly Top panna cotta with a layer of salted caramel sauce, a dollop of crème fraîche (or whipped cream) and a generous sprinkle of hazelnut praline.

Note: Sugar cooks rapidly, is volatile at high temperatures and requires diligent monitoring. Do not step away from the pan.

KINGFISHER OCEANSIDE RESORT & SPA

Richard Benson

For decades, Kingfisher was a best-kept secret destination for Islanders, a casual place with a spectacular view across Baynes Sound. Now the secret is out, in large part due to the impressive multi-million-dollar enhancements made to the property by owner Bill Brandes. The Pacific Mist Spa, with its unique hydropath, and the gorgeous Serenity Gardens in the courtyard have become major attractions. But so has executive chef Richard Benson's West Coast contemporary cuisine at the elevated Ocean7 Restaurant and hip AQUA Bistro & Wine Bar.

Benson, who joined the Kingfisher team in 2015, was promoted to his dream job of executive chef two years later. "I love it, love it, love it," says Benson. He and his wife Sheri have become part of the community, but more than that, the incredible products of the Comox Valley feed both his cooking and his soul.

His biggest producer is Pattison Farms in Black Creek, an organic farm run by Gerry Pattison and his wife, Dagma. "Fantastic man, fantastic products. What he has coming out of the ground is what I'm buying from him," Benson says. Then there's the Out Landish Shellfish Guild, a co-operative of shellfish farmers. "Out Landish is able to grade their own products so the turnaround is much faster. I buy my oysters exclusively from them. The size of the black pearl oyster is just perfect."

All these incredible local products end up in casual dishes like moules frites or the pistachio and pickled beet salad at the New York–style bar AQUA. Meanwhile, Ocean7 provides a fine-dining atmosphere with breathtaking views from every table. "Ocean7 is a destination. It's a special occasion retreat. I want to provide something our guests can't have at home, such as our signature seafood towers," he says. "That's where I believe memories are created."

Wild Pacific Salmon Crudo

SERVES 4 At Ocean7 Restaurant, executive chef Richard Benson makes the most of fresh local seafood, enhancing wild Pacific salmon with the piquant flavours of citrus, avocado, pickled red onion, radish, salmon roe and fresh herbs.

Pickled red onions
2 red onions, thinly sliced (preferably with a mandoline)

4 cups organic apple cider vinegar

½ cup sugar, plus extra depending on desired sweetness

6 black peppercorns

4 bay leaves

3 to 4 sprigs thyme

1 Tbsp coriander seeds

1 Tbsp fennel seeds

½ tsp yellow mustard seeds

Salt, to taste

Salmon crudo
2 Tbsp lemon juice

1 Tbsp orange juice

1 Tbsp grapefruit juice

5 Tbsp extra-virgin olive oil

1 (1-lb) sushi-grade wild Pacific salmon fillet

1 ripe avocado

6 radishes, thinly sliced and chilled in cold water

Pickled Red Onions (see here)

Black pepper

Coarse sea salt, to taste

2 Tbsp chopped dill

2 Tbsp chopped Italian parsley

1 to 2 oz salmon roe

Pickled red onions Place onions into a non-reactive (glass or plastic) container and set aside.

Combine remaining ingredients in a large saucepan and bring to a boil. Remove from heat and let steep for 1 hour. Strain liquid through a fine-mesh sieve over onions. Refrigerate until needed. (Pickled onions can be stored in an airtight container in the fridge for up to 2 weeks.)

Salmon crudo In a small bowl, whisk together lemon, orange and grapefruit juices. Whisk in oil.

Place salmon on a clean cutting board. Using a very sharp knife, thinly slice salmon against the grain and off the skin. Place slices into a glass baking dish. Cover with plastic wrap directly on the slices. Using a flat dish, press down on the salmon pieces until they are flattened and spread out as a very thin layer. Remove plastic and pour in citrus mixture. Refrigerate for 15 minutes.

Pit avocado and thinly slice. Drain radishes. Evenly distribute salmon on 4 plates. Drizzle leftover liquid overtop, then season with salt and pepper. Artfully top salmon with avocado, radishes, pickled red onions, dill, parsley and salmon roe. Serve immediately.

Note: Unlike canning, which creates an environment where micro-organisms cannot grow, quick pickling is a short-term preservation process. Quick pickles must be refrigerated and consumed within a few weeks, and no more than 2 weeks for onions, garlic or mushrooms, which are especially susceptible to food-borne illnesses.

Sea Scallops with Gnocchi and Celeriac Two Ways

SERVES 4 Rich scallops, celeriac, beets, apples, chanterelles: this recipe from Kingfisher resort executive chef Richard Benson makes the most of some of the Island's greatest ingredients in a luxe dish that's ideal for a dinner-party main. Note that you will need to start this dish a day before you serve it as the pickled vegetables need to rest overnight in the fridge. The gnocchi can also be prepared a day or two ahead, making things easier during the main event.

Pickled apples, beets and chanterelles

2 cups chanterelle mushrooms, cleaned and trimmed

1 Granny Smith apple, peeled

2 cooked beets, peeled

Pickled Red Onions pickling liquid (page 94), warm

Gnocchi

1 cup salt, for baking potatoes on

2 russet potatoes, unpeeled

1 egg

1 egg yolk

½ tsp salt

1 cup grated Parmesan

1½ to 2 cups Italian "00" or all-purpose flour, plus extra for dusting

2 Tbsp vegetable oil

Apple cider gastrique

1 cup sugar

1 cup organic apple cider vinegar

¾ tsp coriander seeds

¾ tsp fennel seeds

¼ tsp yellow mustard seeds

4 black peppercorns

2 bay leaves

Pickled apples, beets and chanterelles Place mushrooms in a non-reactive container.

Using a melon baller, create apple spheres and put them into a separate container. Repeat with the beets, into a third container.

Pour in enough warm pickling liquid to cover the beets, mushrooms and apples. Refrigerate overnight.

Note: Unlike canning, which creates an environment where micro-organisms cannot grow, quick pickling is a short-term preservation process. Quick pickles must be refrigerated and consumed within a few weeks, and no more than 2 weeks for onions, garlic or mushrooms, which are especially susceptible to food-borne illnesses.

Gnocchi Preheat oven to 375°F. Cover a baking sheet with salt and set aside.

Pierce potatoes with a paring knife, then arrange potatoes on top of the salt (this helps with the texture of the potato). Bake for 30 to 45 minutes, until potatoes are fork tender.

Halve potatoes lengthwise, scoop out flesh and put through a food mill or vegetable ricer. Transfer to a large bowl.

Add egg, egg yolk, the ½ tsp salt, Parmesan and 1½ cups flour and mix until texture is similar to a soft cookie dough.

If necessary, add more flour. Do not overmix—developing too much gluten will create tough gnocchi.

Line a baking sheet with parchment paper, dust with flour and set aside. On a lightly floured work surface, roll out dough by hand into a rope with a ½-inch diameter. Cut rope into 1-inch pieces. Place gnocchi on the prepared baking sheet and cover until ready to use.

Bring a large saucepan of salted water to a boil. Drop gnocchi into the water and cook for 2 to 3 minutes, until they float to the surface. Using a slotted spoon, transfer gnocchi to a bowl. (Don't dump or strain them or they will be crushed!) Add oil and toss. Transfer gnocchi to the prepared baking sheet, spread out and set aside to cool.

Gnocchi can be made up to 2 days in advance and reheated by pan-frying them in olive oil and/or butter until golden brown.

Apple cider gastrique Place sugar in a saucepan and cook over medium-high heat for 5 minutes, carefully swirling pan to evenly caramelize as it melts, until it is an amber colour. Do not stir.

Carefully add remaining ingredients (as mixture will splatter). Reduce heat to medium-low and simmer until reduced by half and syrupy.

Remove from heat and set aside to steep for 30 minutes. Strain through a fine-mesh sieve into a container and set aside.

Celeriac two ways Cut celeriac(s) into a square shape. Cut 12 (1-inch) cubes and set aside. Coarsely chop the rest.

Heat 2 tablespoons butter in a large saucepan over medium heat. Add shallots and garlic and sauté for 3 to 5 minutes, until shallots are softened. Add coarsely chopped celeriac, milk and bay leaf and cook for 30 to 40 minutes, until celeriac is very soft. Remove bay leaf.

Drain celeriac, reserving the liquid. Transfer celeriac to a blender, add just enough of the liquid to blend, and purée until smooth. Gradually add ¼ cup (½ stick) butter in chunks, puréeing until velvety. Season to taste. (Extra cooking liquid can be saved for stock.)

Fill a bowl with ice water and set aside. Bring a saucepan of salted water to a boil. Add celeriac cubes and parboil for 10 to 15 minutes, until tender. Using a slotted spoon, transfer celeriac to the ice bath. Once cool, transfer to a paper towel–lined plate.

Pan-fry the celeriac cubes with remaining 2 tablespoons butter on medium heat until golden and warmed through. Remove from heat and set aside.

Seared sea scallops Heat oil in a frying pan over medium-high heat. Pat scallops dry and season with salt. Place scallops, seasoned-side down, in pan and sear for 1 minute, until a golden-brown crust forms. Flip scallops over and cook for another 1 minute, until medium-rare to medium.

Add butter and thyme. Using a large spoon, baste sauce over scallops for another minute, until they are opaque and spring back when gently pressed. Do not overcook.

Transfer scallops to a plate to briefly rest. Squeeze lemon overtop.

Assembly While you are preparing the scallops, finish the gnocchi by pan-frying in butter over medium-high heat for 3 to 5 minutes, until warmed through.

Place a small amount of celeriac purée on each of 4 plates. Using the back of a spoon, spread the purée to create a smooth, flat and shiny surface.

Arrange scallops, celeriac cubes and gnocchi on and around the purée. Divide the pickled apples, beets and chanterelles between the plates. Spoon gastrique around the outer edges of the purée, then garnish with microgreens. Serve immediately.

Celeriac two ways

1 to 2 celeriacs (celery roots), peeled (1½ lbs)
½ cup (1 stick) cold butter (divided)
2 small shallots, thinly sliced
1 small clove garlic, chopped
2 cups milk
1 bay leaf
Salt, to taste

Seared sea scallops

2 Tbsp olive oil
20 large (U-10) fresh scallops, muscle removed
Salt
2 Tbsp butter
3 to 4 sprigs thyme
1 lemon, cut in half

Assembly

Gnocchi (see here)
1 Tbsp butter
Microgreens, such as bull's blood beet tops, for garnish

LA STELLA TRATTORIA

Ryan Zuvich

Nanaimo can be a tough place to open a restaurant. Traditionally, it was a mill town, a mall town, the kind of town you'd drive through to get somewhere else. But it's also the kind of place that has huge potential, the kind of potential that appeals to a chef like Ryan Zuvich.

Twelve years ago, he'd just returned from Europe and was cooking in Vancouver and getting restless. "Pick any of the good restaurants of that era, and I'm sure I worked there," he says. "It was time for me to go out on my own."

Then his parents moved to Nanaimo, and he and his wife followed them. "In Nanaimo, we could buy the property," he says. Plus, he saw an opportunity for the kind of food he liked to make. "It was all chain restaurants, nothing local, nothing like what was happening in B.C., Canada or the world. There were all these farms doing great stuff, but it was all being shipped away."

They opened Markt Artisan Deli, which turned into the Hilltop Bistro, and two years later they opened their second restaurant, La Stella Trattoria, which specializes in Italian cuisine. "What we wanted with La Stella was a wood-fired oven. We had a custom-built oven made in California and we started making these Neapolitan-style pizzas." Everything is made from scratch, including the pasta, ham, bacon and sausage. "Our pepperoni is a staple. We make an alarming amount of pepperoni."

And since they arrived in Nanaimo, others have followed, many of them hungry for just what Zuvich is cooking. "There's a huge boom right now," he says. "We're invested in Nanaimo, so we're staying."

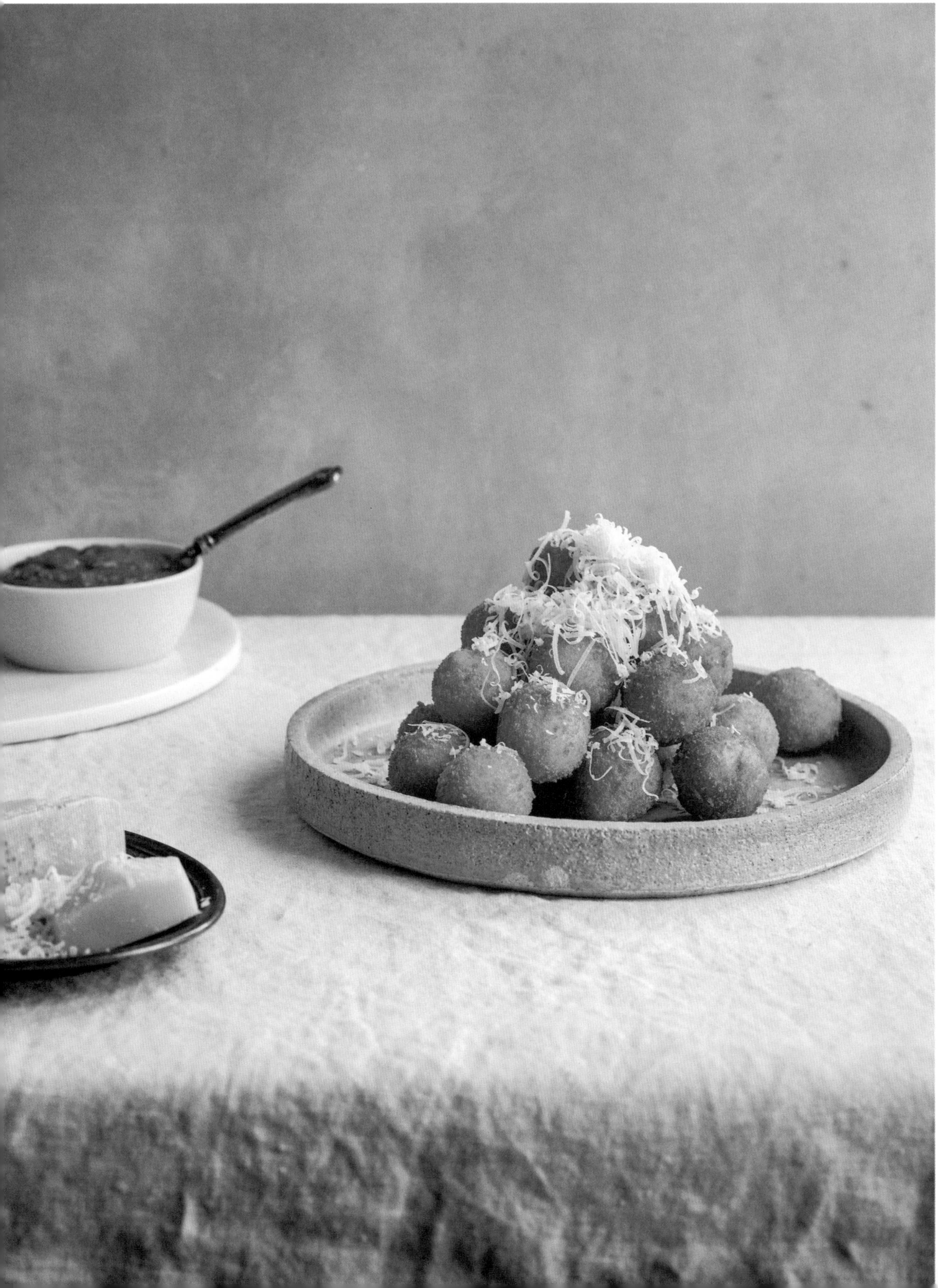

Arancini, p. 100

Arancini

MAKES 12 TO 15 At La Stella Trattoria, chef-owner Ryan Zuvich prepares Italian favourites like these crispy fried rice balls temptingly filled with melty cheese.

4 to 4½ cups vegetable or chicken stock

3 Tbsp olive oil

1 Tbsp butter

1 large shallot, finely chopped

2 cloves garlic, finely chopped

2 cups arborio or carnaroli rice

Juice of ½ lemon, or to taste

½ cup grated Parmesan

Salt, to taste

12 to 15 (½-inch) cubes applewood-smoked cheddar or other cheese of your choice

1 cup flour

2 eggs

2 Tbsp milk

2 cups panko crumbs or bread crumbs

4 cups vegetable oil, for deep-frying

Grated Parmesan (optional), for garnish

Garlic aioli, Bolognese sauce or pesto, to serve

Bring stock to a low simmer in a medium saucepan.

Heat olive oil and butter in a medium saucepan over medium heat, until butter foams. Add shallots and garlic and cook for 5 minutes, until translucent. Add rice and sauté for 2 to 3 minutes, until grains are well coated.

Add 1 cup of warm stock to the rice and stir occasionally, until most of the liquid has been absorbed. Continue adding stock, a cup at time, for 25 minutes, until rice is cooked through and a little bit drier than risotto. Stir in lemon juice. Add Parmesan, then season to taste. Transfer rice to a baking sheet to cool quickly and dry out a bit, which makes it easier to work with.

Using a ¼-cup scoop or large spoon, portion rice into 12 to 15 even-sized balls. Insert a cube of cheese into the centre of each ball, then close up the opening to encapsulate the cheese. Refrigerate uncovered for 30 minutes so the arancini are easier to handle for breading.

Set up a breading station. Place flour in a shallow dish. In a shallow bowl, combine eggs and milk and beat well. Put panko (or bread) crumbs into another dish.

Roll a ball first in the flour, then the egg mixture and the crumbs, making sure to coat well. Place on a baking sheet and repeat with remaining rice balls. (If the arancini are being prepared in advance of a meal, they can be refrigerated until needed. Bring to room temperature for 30 minutes before frying.)

Pour vegetable oil into a deep fryer or deep saucepan and heat to a temperature of 350°F. Carefully lower 2 to 3 arancini into pan, taking care not to splash hot oil. Deep-fry for 5 to 7 minutes, gently turning, until evenly golden. Using a slotted spoon, transfer arancini to a paper towel–lined plate. Keep warm in a 200°F oven and repeat with the remaining arancini.

If you like, sprinkle with grated Parmesan, and serve immediately with garlic aioli, Bolognese sauce or pesto.

Margherita Pizza

SERVES 2 TO 4 Chef Ryan Zuvich brought classic Neapolitan-style pizza to Nanaimo, and Margherita is one of the simplest and best-loved variations. But home cooks can easily experiment with other cheeses and toppings if they wish. Using a pizza stone creates the best product, but if you don't have one, you can use an inverted sheet pan placed on the bottom rack. The recipe yields about two pounds of dough, which is enough for two pizzas. Note that this recipe requires a "biga"—a pre-fermentation starter used in Italian baking to add complexity and texture. It will need to sit for at least half a day before you make your pizza dough.

Biga
⅛ tsp active dry yeast

⅓ cup water, room temperature

1 cup bread flour, Italian "00" flour or a blend

Dough
3½ cups bread flour, Italian "00" flour or a blend, plus extra for dusting

1¼ cups + 1 Tbsp water

½ Tbsp salt

1¼ tsp active dry yeast

Biga (see here)

2 Tbsp extra-virgin olive oil

Assembly
Dough (see here)

Flour, for dusting

1 (798-mL) can San Marzano or plum tomatoes, puréed

2 balls fior di latte (preferably Natural Pastures Cheese Company), sliced

Small bunch basil, leaves only

Sea salt, for sprinkling

Good-quality olive oil, to finish

Biga In a large bowl, combine yeast and water. Add flour and mix until just smooth. Cover with plastic wrap and set aside at room temperature for 12 to 16 hours, until doubled in size and dimpled in the centre.

Dough In a stand mixer fitted with a hook attachment, combine flour, water, salt and yeast. Mix on low speed for 3 minutes until incorporated and dough comes together. Add in biga in chunks, then increase the speed and gradually add oil. Mix until incorporated.

Set dough in bowl aside for 1 hour to proof, uncovered, then transfer to a clean work surface and fold once. Cover and set aside for another hour. The dough should be smooth and soft (it should not be sticky), hold its shape well and stretch easily without tearing.

Gently divide dough into 2 balls. Place the portioned balls on a lightly floured work surface, seam-side down, and lightly dust with flour. Cover with a linen towel (or plastic wrap) and set aside for 20 minutes.

Assembly Place a pizza stone or inverted baking sheet inside oven and preheat oven to 500°F.

Shape each ball of dough into a 12-inch disc and place on a lightly floured wooden surface such as a pizza peel or cutting board that will accommodate the size of the pie. Spread sauce over each one, then arrange slices of fior di latte and basil leaves on top. Give it a little shake on the board to loosen. Transfer pizzas to oven (one at a time, if needed) and bake for 4 to 6 minutes, until cooked through. Remove from oven, then sprinkle with salt and lightly drizzle with oil.

LONG BEACH LODGE RESORT

Shaun Snelling

Tim Hackett fell in love with the untamed beauty of the Island's west coast when he first visited Long Beach in the 1960s, camping on the beach with friends. Decades later, when a property on Cox Bay came up for sale, Hackett snapped it up. "He knew right away that he wanted to build a lodge that resembled a grand beach house," says Samantha Hackett, general manager of Long Beach Lodge Resort and Tim's niece by marriage.

In 2002, the forty-one-room lodge opened its doors, featuring The Great Room overlooking Cox Bay, and became the first Canadian property ever featured in *Architectural Digest*. The lodge has since expanded to include twenty cottages, the Surf Club and Sandbar Bistro. Meanwhile, The Great Room has become one of this coast's best-loved places to sip a glass of wine, dive into a bowl of chowder or just gaze dreamily at the waves of Tofino's best surf beach.

Shaun Snelling has been executive chef here since 2018, cooking up his locally driven, upscale casual fare in The Great Room as well as the seasonal Sandbar Bistro, Tofino's only restaurant right on the beach. In The Great Room, aside from a dinner menu showcasing plenty of local tuna, Dungeness crab and salmon, there's a daily brunch menu and an "après-surf" one featuring flatbreads and small bites. Surf culture is part of the brand, whether a guest hits the waves, hangs out at the Surf Club or just watches the action from a window, hot chocolate in hand.

That is, after all, what The Great Room was designed for. "When the lodge opened, and even now, this is your living room away from home," Hackett says. "It's familiar and comfortable. People can treat themselves when they're here, but it's not pretentious."

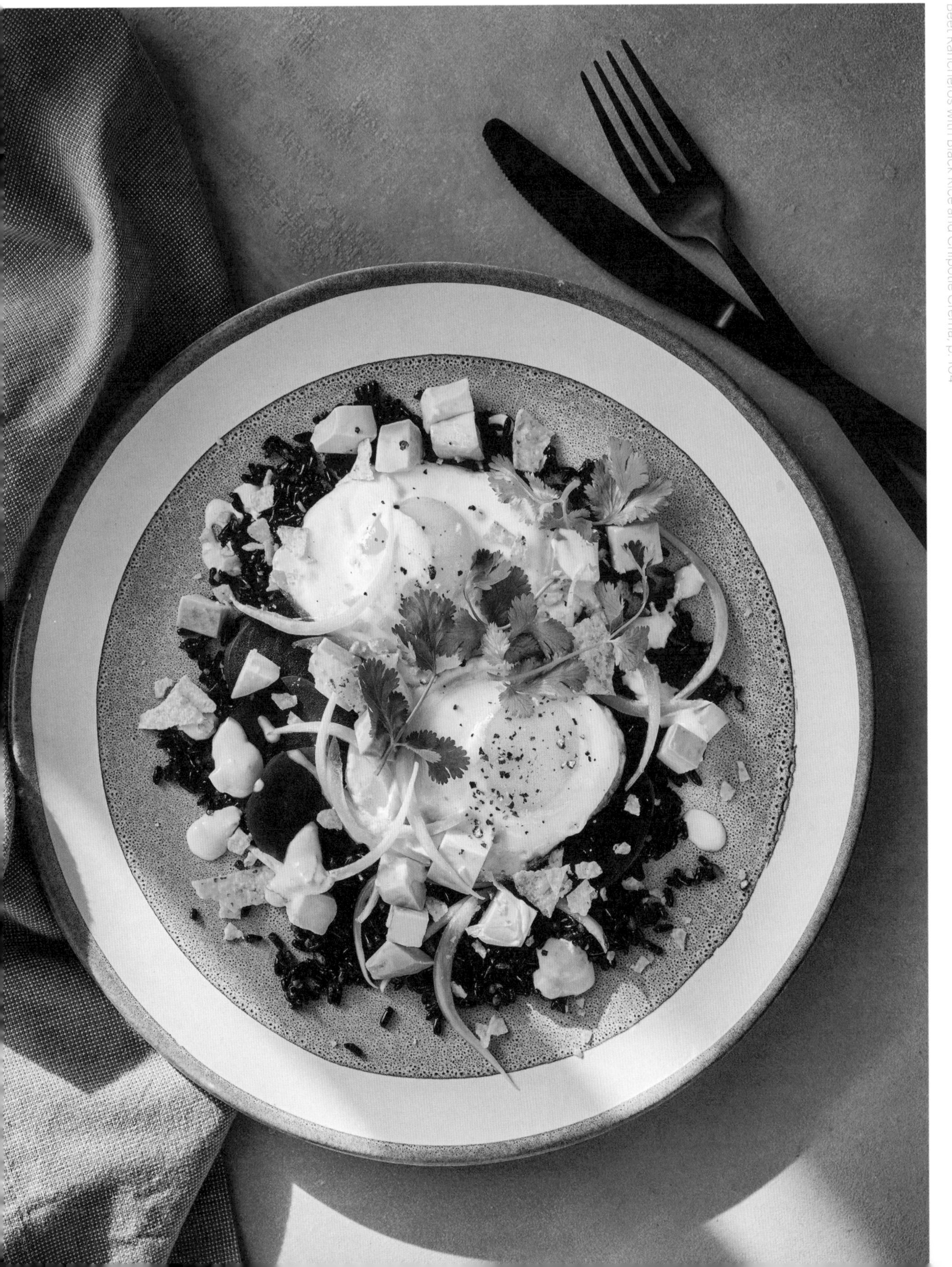

Beet Rancheros with Black Rice and Chipotle Crema, p. 104

Beet Rancheros with Black Rice and Chipotle Crema

SERVES 4 Brunch is served every day at Long Beach Lodge Resort, and there are few more idyllic ways to spend a lazy morning than sitting in The Great Room, watching the waves and enjoying chef Shaun Snelling's fine fare. That includes this popular Mexican-accented dish. The pickled onions are also great in tacos and salads. And if you can't find black rice, brown rice or farro would be a good substitute.

Pickled onions
1 cup red wine vinegar
1 cup water
½ cup sugar
2 tsp salt
1 large red onion, thinly sliced

Beets
4 to 5 beets
1 Tbsp cumin seeds
1 Tbsp coriander seeds
1 Tbsp smoked paprika
1 Tbsp salt
Bunch of cilantro stems

Rice
2 cups black rice
1 tsp ground cumin
1 tsp smoked paprika

Chipotle crema
1 cup sour cream
Grated zest and juice
   of ½ lime
Small bunch of cilantro,
   leaves only, chopped
2 Tbsp chopped chipotles
   in adobo

Assembly
2 avocados, thinly sliced
8 eggs
Crumbled tortilla chips,
   for garnish
Cilantro leaves, for garnish

Pickled onions In a small saucepan, combine vinegar, water, sugar and salt and bring to a boil. Remove from heat.

Place onions in a non-reactive, heat-proof dish and pour hot pickling liquid overtop. Set aside to cool and refrigerate until needed. (It can be stored in an airtight container in the fridge for 2 weeks.)

Beets In a medium saucepan, combine all ingredients and enough water to cover. Bring to a boil and then simmer on medium-low for 20 to 40 minutes, until beets are fork tender. Drain and set beets aside until cool enough to handle.

Using a paper towel, rub off skins. Slice beets into ½-inch-thick rounds. Set aside.

Rice In a saucepan, combine all ingredients, add enough water and cook according to package directions. Set aside and keep warm.

Chipotle crema Combine all of the ingredients in a bowl and mix well.

Assembly Preheat oven to 375°F.

Place beets in a baking dish and warm up in oven for 5 minutes.

Prepare eggs how you'd like them: e.g., poached, scrambled or sunny-side up.

Divide rice among 4 plates, then top with beets, avocado and eggs. Drizzle chipotle crema overtop and garnish with pickled onions, crumbled chips and cilantro.

Seared Albacore Tuna with Apple Slaw and Sweet Onion Purée

SERVES 4 Albacore tuna is one of the great sustainable seafoods from this coast. Long Beach Lodge's executive chef Shaun Snelling advises that since the tuna is purchased frozen, it will need to be thawed before it's cooked. Shichimi togarashi—a zingy combination of citrus, chili and nori—can be found in gourmet stores, specialty markets and online.

Sweet onion purée
1 Tbsp canola oil
2 sweet onions, chopped
1 cup natural pickled ginger
1 cup water
2 tsp fish sauce

Tuna
1 (1-lb) cleaned albacore or ahi tuna loin
Shichimi togarashi, to taste
Salt, to taste
1 Tbsp canola or grapeseed oil

Apple slaw
2 Granny Smith apples, peeled
½ daikon radish, peeled, or 4 radishes
½ head green cabbage, quartered and thinly sliced
½ bunch green onions, chopped
½ bunch cilantro, chopped
Juice of 1 lime
1 Tbsp sugar
2 tsp tamari or soy sauce

Sweet onion purée Heat oil in a small saucepan over medium heat. Add onions and sauté for 10 minutes, until softened and translucent. Add pickled ginger and water, bring back to a boil, then cover and reduce heat to low. Cook for 15 minutes.

Transfer to a blender or food processor and blend until smooth. Stir in fish sauce and refrigerate for at least 2 hours, until chilled.

Tuna Pat tuna dry and lightly season on all sides with shichimi togarashi and salt.

Heat oil in a large frying pan over high heat. Carefully add tuna and sear for 20 seconds on each side. Transfer to a plate, then refrigerate for at least 30 minutes, until chilled.

Apple slaw Using a Japanese mandoline with the teeth attachment, carefully grate apples and daikon (or radishes). (Alternatively, cut into thin matchsticks.)

Combine the apples, radishes, cabbage, onions and cilantro in a bowl. In a separate bowl, combine lime juice, sugar and tamari (or soy sauce). Pour dressing over slaw and mix well. Set aside.

Assembly Thinly slice tuna and serve with apple slaw and sweet onion purée.

THE MAHLE HOUSE RESTAURANT

Stephen Wilson and Luke Griffin

These days, Stephen Wilson likes to joke about the "all-expenses-paid" wedding his wife Tara's family gave the couple at their place outside Nanaimo. "I didn't realize when I got a free wedding in 2000, I'd have to buy the restaurant years later," he says with a laugh.

That restaurant is the Mahle House, a neighbourhood favourite in the rural community of Cedar since it opened in 1983. "My mother-in-law Maureen and her brother Delbert bought the house in the 1970s from the Mahle family, who had been in the neighbourhood since the 1800s. The restaurant building was built in 1904," Wilson says. When Maureen and Delbert retired in 2009, the Wilsons—who'd worked at some of Victoria's best restaurants, including the beloved (and now-shuttered) Camille's—took it over.

Since then, Wilson has planted a large and productive kitchen garden, and added heritage pigs and chickens for eggs. "I've been farming more than I've been cooking this year," he says. "I start getting radishes and arugula in April, and I still get beets, carrots and kale through December."

They've also updated the menu, with the help of chef Luke Griffin, who is originally from Toronto but has been at the Mahle House for four years now. Among other things, he's responsible for making terrines, rillettes and dry-cured ham. "We don't specify ourselves as having one kind of cuisine," Griffin says, adding that they use whatever is in season, and there is plenty to choose from: truffles, berries, seafood. "We play with whatever we can get our hands on. We make everything in-house."

With every passing season, Wilson is more and more glad his not-so-free wedding brought him to Cedar. "I just love the rural nature and tight community."

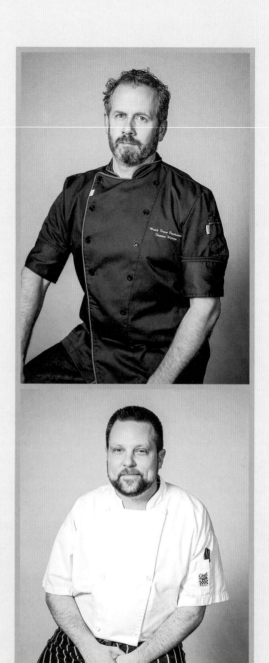

Pork Ravioli with Lemon and Cherry Tomatoes

SERVES 4 (AS A FIRST COURSE) The Mahle House's chef Luke Griffin advises that home cooks can use just about any filling they like—as long as it's not too wet or crumbly—and that this works as either an appetizer or an entrée.

Pasta dough

3⅔ cups semolina flour, all-purpose flour or Italian "00" flour, plus extra for dusting

1 Tbsp olive oil

1 tsp salt

5 eggs

Filling

1 Tbsp vegetable oil

12 oz ground pork

2 Tbsp chopped thyme

2 Tbsp garlic powder

2 Tbsp onion powder

1 Tbsp crushed red pepper

1 tsp salt

1 tsp black pepper

Assembly

Flour, for dusting

¼ cup olive oil (divided)

2 Tbsp butter

12 to 16 cherry tomatoes

2 tsp grated lemon zest

¼ cup chopped herbs and greens, such as basil, Italian parsley or arugula, plus extra for garnish (optional)

Crushed red pepper (optional)

Salt, to taste

Good-quality grated Parmesan

Microgreens, for garnish

Pasta dough On a clean work surface, shape flour into a mound. Make a well in the centre, then add oil, salt and eggs. Use a fork to stir the eggs and then gradually incorporate flour to form a dough. Knead for 5 to 7 minutes, until dough is smooth and pliable and springs back to shape when gently pressed. (You need to be able to fold and shape the dough to hold the filling. If it is too sticky, add a little flour. If too dry, add a splash of water or olive oil.)

Wrap dough ball tightly in plastic wrap and set aside to rest at room temperature for 1 hour. If you are not using it right away, the dough will keep for a couple days in the fridge or for a month in the freezer when tightly wrapped.

Filling Heat oil in a frying pan over medium-high heat. Add pork and cook for 10 minutes, stirring occasionally, until cooked through. Drain, then transfer to a bowl. Add remaining ingredients and mix well. Set aside to cool, then refrigerate until needed.

Assembly Divide the dough into 4 equal pieces. Flatten each piece into a rectangle ½ inch thick with a floured rolling pin. Cover any unused portion with a dish towel or plastic wrap until needed. Roll the pieces of dough through a pasta machine, starting with the thickest setting and working to the thinnest, until each sheet is ⅛ inch thick and slightly translucent. (Alternatively, roll out the dough using a rolling pin.)

Place a length of pasta dough on a lightly floured work surface, making sure it is 6 inches wide. Mentally cut the sheet in half lengthwise and then imagine a divider every 3 inches along the lower sheet. Starting 1½ inches from the left, place heaped tablespoons of filling along the lower half of the dough, evenly spacing them 3 inches apart. Using a pastry brush and a small bowl of water, lightly brush the pasta sheet around the filling. Carefully fold the top half sheet over the filling, using your fingers to press out air and avoid creating any air pockets. Using a knife or pizza roller, cut ravioli and tightly press all edges together to ensure a complete seal. Be careful not to stretch and tear the dough. Repeat with the other three lengths. You should end up with about 24 ravioli.

Dust a baking sheet with flour. Place ravioli on the prepared baking sheet, cover with a dish towel and refrigerate until needed.

(Ravioli can freeze well. Simply place the baking sheet of ravioli in the freezer and freeze until hardened. Transfer ravioli to a container or freezer bag and freeze until needed.)

Bring a large pot of lightly salted water to a boil. Working in batches to avoid over-crowding (and prevent sticking), gently lower 3 to 4 ravioli into the water. Cook for 3 to 4 minutes (or allow an extra minute if cooking from frozen). Using a slotted spoon, gently transfer cooked ravioli to a baking sheet and repeat with the remainder.

Heat 2 tablespoons oil in each of 2 large frying pans over medium-high heat, until oil is "dancing." Gently lower 3 to 4 ravioli into each pan, taking care not to splash yourself with hot oil.

Lightly shake pans, and add a knob of butter to each. Divide tomatoes, lemon zest, herbs and crushed red pepper (if using) between the 2 pans. Cook for 20 seconds, shaking pans, then turn ravioli over and cook for another 30 seconds, until tomatoes have burst. Season to taste. Repeat with remaining ravioli.

Transfer ravioli and tomatoes to 4 shallow bowls or plates. Drizzle pan juices overtop, then sprinkle with Parmesan. Garnish with fresh herbs (if using) and microgreens.

Crème Brûlée Napoleon

If there is one dessert that will never leave the Mahle House's menu, it's this twist on the classic crème brûlée. Make all the components the day before so the caramel and custard have time to set, then assemble just before serving.

Caramel sauce

1 cup sugar
2 Tbsp water
1 cup whipping (33%) cream
1 tsp vanilla extract

Phyllo rectangles

1 cup sugar
1 cup pecans
2 sheets phyllo pastry
¼ cup (½ stick) butter, melted

Custard

3 cups whipping (33%) cream
1 vanilla bean, split lengthwise,
    or 1 Tbsp vanilla extract
⅔ cup sugar
7 egg yolks

Caramel sauce Combine sugar and water in a small heavy-bottomed saucepan and bring to a simmer over medium heat, until light amber. Do not stir.

Remove pan from heat. Carefully add cream and stir for a minute, until fully incorporated and smooth. (Be careful as mixture will bubble vigorously.) If the sauce appears lumpy, return pan to medium heat and stir until smooth. Stir in vanilla and set aside.

(Leftover sauce can be refrigerated in an airtight container for up to 2 weeks. To serve, set aside at room temperature for 2 hours to soften or heat over medium-low heat until slightly warmed through.)

Phyllo rectangles Preheat oven to 350°F. Line a baking sheet with parchment paper.

Combine sugar and pecans in a food processor and process until pecans are reduced to the size of quinoa. Do not over-process. Reserve ¼ cup for garnish.

With the long side of the phyllo in front of you, cut each sheet vertically in half. You should have 4 equal-sized rectangles. (We only need 3 rectangles for the recipe. The fourth can be reserved for another use.)

Place a rectangle on the prepared baking sheet and brush with butter. Generously sprinkle pecan mixture overtop. Add 2 more layers of phyllo, butter and pecans.

Using a pizza roller or sharp knife, carefully cut stacked phyllo into 12 even rectangles, roughly 2½ × 4½ inches, making sure they are separated slightly and not stuck together. Bake for 7 to 8 minutes, until lightly golden brown. Set aside to cool. (They can be stored in an airtight container for 1 to 2 days.)

Custard Preheat oven to 325°F. You'll need a 9-inch round cake pan or 9 x 9-inch cake pan that will fit into a larger roasting pan.

Combine cream and vanilla bean (if using vanilla extract, do not add yet) in a medium saucepan and bring it to just below a boil over medium heat. Quickly remove from heat and set aside for 15 minutes to infuse flavour. Remove vanilla bean.

In a medium bowl, whisk eggs and sugar together until smooth.

Very slowly drizzle hot cream into eggs, stirring constantly. (This tempers the eggs and prevents them from cooking. Add vanilla extract now, if using.)

Strain egg mixture through a fine-mesh sieve into a cake pan to remove any cooked egg but retain vanilla seeds. Place into a roasting pan and fill with hot water halfway up the cake pan sides. Cover roasting pan with aluminum foil and use a sharp knife to pierce with a few holes to allow steam to escape. Bake 40 to 45 minutes, until custard is just set. It should be jiggly, but not runny, in the centre. Set aside for 1 hour, until completely cooled. Cover in plastic wrap and refrigerate overnight. (Do not let the wrap come into contact with the custard.)

Assembly Fit a piping bag with a round or star tip and fill halfway with custard. (Alternatively, use a large spoon.) Squeeze or spoon a couple tablespoons of custard onto each of 4 plates, which will be used to anchor the phyllo.

Place a phyllo rectangle on each plate, atop the custard base. Pipe or spoon a generous layer of custard onto the rectangles. If the custard is properly cooked it will be just thick enough to hold its shape without running and also show the pattern of the piping tip.

Place another rectangle on each stack, pressing down gently (don't squeeze custard out, just make it level). Pipe a layer of custard on top. Place a final rectangle on top, again pressing down gently.

Using a squeeze bottle or a small spoon, drizzle a generous amount of caramel sauce over each napoleon. Sprinkle pecan sugar and icing sugar (if using) overtop and on plate as garnish. Finish with candied pecans, berries and mint (if using).

Assembly

¼ cup reserved pecan sugar from Phyllo Rectangles (see here)

Icing sugar, for sprinkling (Optional)

Candied pecans, for garnish (optional)

Berries, for garnish (optional)

Mint leaves, for garnish (optional)

MELANGE
Kellie Callender

Kellie Callender has cooked in Bhutan, Vietnam, India, China and Whistler, where he was the chef for Canadian athletes training for the 2014 Winter Olympics. He's motorbiked across Vietnam from Ho Chi Minh City to Hanoi, trained with the Ghanaian national judo team in Accra and eaten his way through Spain, France, Japan and Israel.

But now he's living perhaps his biggest adventure right here in his hometown of Nanaimo, operating a restaurant amidst a scene that's just starting to evolve. "The downtown core has changed a lot in the last three years," Callender says. "People who come into the restaurant don't expect this type of restaurant to be in Nanaimo, but they're stoked that it's here."

A "melange" is a mixture or medley of things, and that describes Callender's cuisine to a T. The menu features mainly globetrotting small plates, such as the gochujang tuna tostada or sushi-like Jubei's Dragon Ball (page 114). "That comes from travelling," he says. "And my favourite restaurants in Nanaimo are all Asian restaurants. There's a good diversity of cultures here."

Returning home, he's been excited by the impeccable local ingredients he's discovered, from Gabriola Island beef to sturgeon farmed at Vancouver Island University to wild mushrooms from nearby forests. He now works with over fifteen farmers and foragers, and has collaborated with filmmaker Cam MacArthur and Ecologyst on the Food Tastes Better Outside series, educating people about the importance of sustainable fishing.

"One of my main goals is to keep the money in the local community. We won't sell any animal protein that isn't coming from the Island," he says. "It's turning into a real community and it'll only continue to grow."

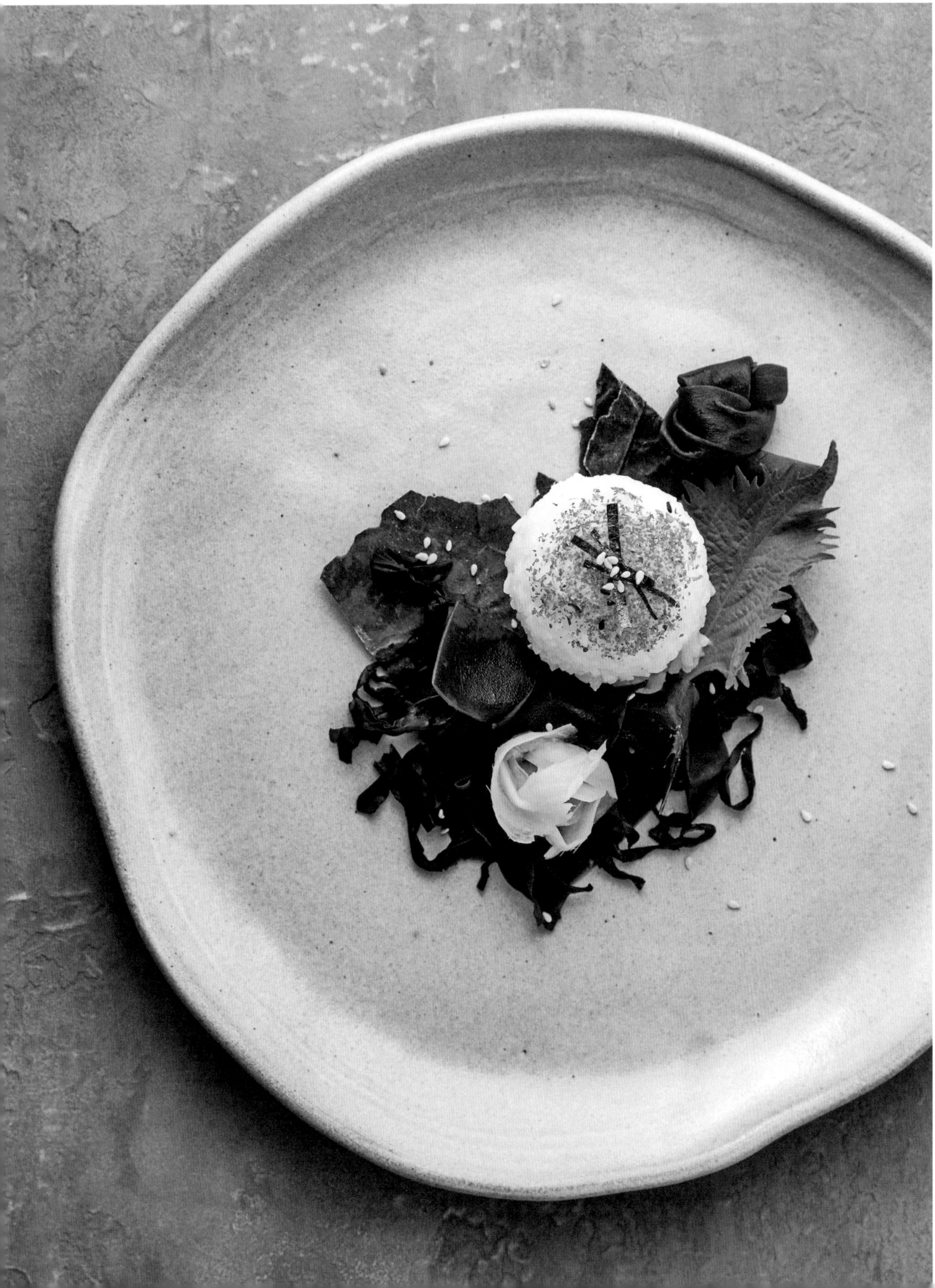

Jubei's Dragon Ball, p. 114

Jubei's Dragon Ball

SERVES 4 TO 6 At Nanaimo's Melange Restaurant, chef-owner Kellie Callender typically makes this spherical take on sushi vegan, but he says you can fill it with whatever you wish, such as raw or smoked seafood, for instance. "Basically choose two ingredients you think go well together and mix them with the miso paste," he says.

The dish is named for an anime character who opened a film eating a similar rice ball. Callender believes that "the beauty of cooking rice is allowing it to teach you to make it the way you like. A little extra water will create a softer texture, a little less results in something firmer."

Sushi vinegar

¼ cup rice vinegar or red wine vinegar

2 Tbsp sugar

2 tsp salt

Sushi rice

2 cups sushi rice

2½ to 3 cups water, depending on how soft you like your rice

Sushi Vinegar (see here), reserving 1 to 2 tsp for miso-sesame paste

Miso-sesame paste

3 Tbsp miso

3 Tbsp sesame seeds

1 to 2 tsp Sushi Vinegar (see here) or sake

Filling options

Apple and roasted garlic

Chopped cashews and fresh ginger

Napa cabbage and thinly sliced red onion

Sautéed wild mushrooms and shallots

Garnish options

Aioli

Chilled vegetable purée

Kecap manis (Indonesian sweet soy sauce)

Kimchi

Nori, cut into smaller squares or thin strips

Pickled ginger

Pickled mushrooms

Salad greens

Shichimi togarashi or gochugaru (mild Korean chili flakes)

Toasted nuts or seeds

Wasabi

Sushi vinegar In a small bowl, combine all ingredients and mix well. It should taste balanced and intense.

Sushi rice Rinse rice in a fine-mesh sieve under cold running water until the water runs clear. Combine rice and water in a medium saucepan and bring to a boil. Reduce heat to low, cover and cook for 20 minutes, until rice is tender. Gently mix in the sushi vinegar, then set aside to cool to room temperature.

Note: Do not refrigerate the rice—it will make this process more challenging and the dish won't taste nearly as good. Any leftover rice can be used for fried rice or congee (rice porridge).

Miso-sesame paste Using a mortar and pestle, combine miso and sesame seeds until a paste forms. Add 1 teaspoon sushi vinegar (or sake) to create a spreadable paste. Add more if needed.

Mix your choice of filling with a little miso-sesame paste so that it tastes slightly salty.

Assembly Wet your hands so you can handle the sticky rice. Scoop out ⅓ cup to ½ cup of rice (depending on how big you want the ball) and form a patty in the palm of your hand. Slowly round up the edges while pressing the centre so it remains hollow. Place a tablespoon of filling in the centre of the rice, then round the rice edge over the filling until a ball is formed, adding more rice if needed. Position the ball on the plate with the smoothest side facing up. Add your desired garnishes.

Note: You can make a sweet variation by omitting the miso paste and replacing it with sweet red bean paste and cacao nibs. You could also use apple or pear compote, or even apricot marmalade and small-diced melon. Sweet garnishes include fruit purée, fruit compote or shaved melon with honey and salt.

Borja's Spanish-Style Cheesecake

SERVES 8 Chef Kellie Callender learned to make this classic Spanish-style cheesecake from a man named Borja, whom he met while running a restaurant on Gabriola Island, and then again in Borja's hometown of San Sebastián. "Now I'm sharing it with you," Callender says. "Great cooking is developed through connections with people and places."

2 cups cream cheese, room temperature

1 cup sugar

4 eggs

1 cup whipping (33%) cream or heavy (36%) cream

1 Tbsp flour

Preheat oven to 400°F. Line the bottom and sides of a 10-inch springform pan with parchment paper, crumpling the parchment a little so it is easy to form into the pan.

In a stand mixer fitted with a paddle attachment, cream the cream cheese and sugar together at medium-low speed. With the motor running, add eggs, one at a time, and mix well after each addition. Slowly pour in cream. Sift in flour and mix.

Pour batter into the prepared pan and bake for 35 to 40 minutes, until set but still a bit jiggly in the centre.

If desired, preheat a broiler and then broil for 2 to 3 minutes, until the top has caramelized. Set aside to cool to room temperature, then refrigerate overnight to set completely.

OUEST ARTISAN PATISSERIE

Jessyca Fulsom and Stephen Nason

"I like to say that first you eat with your eyes, so food should be beautiful," says Jessyca Fulsom. "And then it should taste as good as it looks." That's as good a description as any of the works of art she and her partner, chef Stephen Nason, offer at their Tofino pastry shop.

The duo met in 2013 in Kelowna, where Nason was working at a French patisserie after running his own, La Bamboche, in Toronto. "In Toronto, Stephen was one of the first chefs to introduce Japanese flavours to pastry, so he was ground-breaking," Fulsom says. "We still have a lot of Asian influence in our flavours." She, on the other hand, had worked in retail management, studied art at university and turned her skills to hand-painted cookies and fondant flowers.

Fulsom, who'd grown up in Nanoose Bay, always wanted to return home. She toured Nason all over the Island, searching for a place to set up shop. "The last place I brought Stephen was to Tofino. It was all part of my plan," she says. "It's hard not to fall in love with Tofino."

They opened in April 2020, at the very end of the town's main road. "People feel like they've discovered their secret place," Fulsom says. They do traditional French patisserie and viennoiserie—macarons, croissants, choux—and wedding cakes. ("Tofino has a crazy amount of weddings," Fulsom says.) And remarkably, everything is produced from an eight-by-twenty converted shipping container with open doors, terrible climate control, very limited space and basically no storage. Every time the weather changes, they have to quickly adapt.

"We love Tofino because people are very open to cool flavour combinations," she says. "The classics are still popular, but it's fun to know that if you make a brown butter and sage macaron, people will still be talking about it three months later."

Blackberry–Earl Grey Jam

MAKES 5 TO 6 (250-ML) JARS Jessyca Fulsom, co-owner of Ouest Patisserie in Tofino, advises using a good quality loose-leaf tea in this jam. "Double Cream Earl Grey from Thay Tea in Ucluelet is, by far, our favourite," she says. Note that you will need canning tools for making the jam, including six 250-mL Mason jars with snap lids and rings, a ladle, a funnel and a candy thermometer. Fulsom says using this natural jam method creates a softer set.

2 lbs blackberries
4 cups sugar
Juice of 1 lemon
½ cup boiling water
5 tsp loose Earl Grey tea
 leaves

Combine blackberries, sugar and lemon juice in a large, deep saucepan. Set aside for 2 hours at room temperature to macerate.

Preheat oven to 250°F.

In a bowl, combine tea leaves and boiling water and set aside for 10 minutes to steep. Strain through a fine-mesh sieve into another bowl, then set aside.

Cook berry mixture over medium-high heat until it reaches a measure of 221°F. (This high temperature is very important in order to set the jam.) Stir in tea and boil for 1 minute, then remove from heat.

Pour into sterilized jars, leaving a ½-inch headspace. Make sure rims are immaculate, then place snap lids on jars and loosely add rings until just finger tight.

Place sealed jars on a clean baking sheet and put in the oven for 20 minutes. Remove from oven, leave on the baking sheet and cool to room temperature. As they cool, you should hear a "ping" sound, which indicates the jars have sealed. Any jars that don't seal should be stored in the refrigerator.

Note: The oven method is Ouest's preferred canning technique and is a clean, simple method of preserving jam. However, done improperly, it can be dangerous for a home cook. If you want, you can use a traditional water bath instead. Once you've placed the sterilized snap lids and rings on the jars of hot jam, submerge them in boiling water for 10 minutes, then remove to cool. In either case, listen for the ping that indicates the jars have sealed, and store any unsealed jars of jam in the fridge.

Paris-Brest

MAKES 12 PASTRIES Paris-Brest, a traditional French dessert named for a famous bicycle race, has not changed much since debuting in 1910, but has recently seen a surge in popularity—with creative new takes on the original. The marriage of choux and praline-flavoured cream makes this one of the bestselling desserts at Ouest Patisserie.

Pastry cream

3 egg yolks
¼ cup sugar
1½ Tbsp cornstarch
1 cup milk
1 tsp vanilla paste or extract
1½ Tbsp butter, room temperature

Choux

½ cup milk
½ cup water
1 tsp salt
1 tsp sugar
½ cup (1 stick) butter, cut into cubes
1 cup flour
4 eggs
½ cup sliced almonds

Assembly

1 cup store-bought sweetened praline paste
½ cup (1 stick) butter, cubed, room temperature
Pastry Cream (see here), chilled
Choux (see here)
Icing sugar, for sprinkling

Pastry cream Combine egg yolks and sugar in a medium bowl and whisk until pale yellow and creamy. Whisk in cornstarch. Set aside.

In a medium saucepan, combine milk and vanilla and bring just below a boil over medium heat. Quickly remove from heat. Slowly and gradually pour hot milk into the egg mixture, whisking constantly until smooth.

Transfer mixture back to saucepan and cook over medium-low heat until gently simmering, while whisking constantly to prevent eggs from scrambling. Whisk in butter until incorporated.

Remove from heat and transfer to a clean bowl. Cover with plastic wrap, pressing it directly onto the cream's surface to prevent a skin from forming. Set aside to cool to room temperature. Refrigerate for at least 2 hours, until chilled. Preheat oven to 350°F (or a convection oven to 325°F). On 2 sheets of parchment paper, use a pencil to draw 12 circles, 2½ inches in diameter and equally spaced 2 inches apart. (You will use this to trace your "wheels" later.) Line 2 baking sheets with the parchment, pencil side down.

Choux Combine milk, water, salt, sugar and butter in a saucepan and bring to a lively boil over medium heat. Remove from stove. Add flour and mix with a spatula. Reduce heat to low and return pan to stove, stirring constantly, for 2 minutes until dough reaches 175°F and comes off the sides of the pan.

Place dough in a stand mixer fitted with a paddle attachment. Mix on low speed for 5 to 10 minutes, until dough is smooth and cooled to 125°F.

Add eggs, one at a time, beating each fully into the batter before adding the next.

Fit a piping bag with a round tip and scrape dough into the bag. Pipe open circles of dough on the parchment-lined baking sheets, following the "bicycle wheel" templates you drew earlier.

Liberally sprinkle with sliced almonds. Bake for 25 to 30 minutes, until a deep golden colour. (Note: The depth of colour is important; undercooked choux is not airy or hollow inside.) Remove from oven and set aside to cool completely.

Assembly In a stand mixer fitted with a whisk attachment, beat praline paste and butter together for 5 minutes, until smooth. Add chilled pastry cream and blend until just combined.

Carefully slice each choux ring in half horizontally. Fit a piping bag with a star tip and fill with praline filling. Pipe mixture onto bottom half of the ring, making small rosettes or spiralling all the way around. Close with top of the ring and dust with icing sugar. Repeat with remaining choux rings. Keep refrigerated and serve at room temperature.

Note: The pastry cream and unfilled choux may be made ahead of time. They can be stored in separate airtight containers in the fridge for up to 3 days. Do not incorporate praline until ready to assemble as it will separate.

OXEYE

Josh Blumenthal, Daly Gyles, Nick Gladu

Expect fanatical foodies to make their way to
Galiano Island, small though it is, thanks to a
handful of chefs with Michelin-star expertise and a
passion for remote places.

The leader of the pack is Josh Blumenthal, late
of Bishop's and Wildebeest in Vancouver, Gera-
nium in Copenhagen and Viajante in London. "My
partner and I wanted to get out of the city. We tried
Salt Spring, but it was too big and too busy," he
says. Galiano, it turned out, was just right. "I got
lucky with being able to drag two of my friends to
a small island."

Those friends are Nick Gladu, formerly of Bish-
op's in Vancouver and sous chef of Two Lights in
London, and Daly Gyles, the former sous chef at
London's St. John and Vancouver's Ask for Luigi.
Together the trio is operating Oxeye, a casual café
concept in Sturdies Bay.

"We use all island-based ingredients from Salt
Spring, Galiano and Vancouver Island," Blumenthal says. "We have tons of cool stuff to work with."
That includes nuts, lamb, rabbits, mushrooms, wild
edibles, fresh-milled grains and even kumquats
and Meyer lemons from a farm on Salt Spring
Island. He adds, "The citrus is a big find. Plus the
quality of animals raised on the islands and the
everyday produce are just phenomenal here."

Mainly they serve breakfasts, lunches and
baked goods like their miso-caramel blondie and
buckwheat galettes with seasonal fruit, but they're
planning to host pop-up dinners as well. After all,
you never know who might find their way to this
island in the Salish Sea.

Fresh-Milled Wheat Tagliatelle and Lobster Mushroom Ragout, p. 122

Fresh-Milled Wheat Tagliatelle and Lobster Mushroom Ragout

SERVES 4 TO 6 At Oxeye on Galiano Island, chef-owner Josh Blumenthal and his co-chefs find inspiration in local ingredients, farmed or foraged, like the lobster mushrooms that grow wild in the forests. Freshly milled heritage wheat, like that from True Grain in Cowichan Bay, has a nutty flavour and a toothsome texture.

Pasta

2¾ cups organic durum semolina flour

1¼ cups fine-milled hard spring wheat flour, plus extra for dusting

4 eggs

3 egg yolks

1 Tbsp oil

1 tsp salt

Lobster mushroom ragout

¼ cup grapeseed oil

1 sweet onion, thinly sliced (1 cup)

1 Tbsp salt, or to taste

1 large red bell pepper, seeded, deveined and thinly sliced

2 Tbsp apple cider vinegar

½ cup white wine

4 cups sliced lobster mushrooms or mixed wild mushrooms

1 Tbsp kelp powder (see Note)

Assembly

Edible flowers, for garnish (optional)

Pasta In a stand mixer fitted with a hook attachment, combine flours.

In a separate bowl, whisk together eggs, yolks, oil and salt. Add wet mixture to dry ingredients and mix on low speed until a smooth dough is formed. Transfer dough to a lightly floured work surface and knead for 5 minutes, until dough is smooth and pliable and springs back to shape when gently pressed. Cover with a dish towel or plastic wrap and refrigerate for at least 2 hours.

Bring pasta dough to room temperature. Divide the dough into 4 equal pieces. Flatten each piece into a rectangle ½-inch thick with a floured rolling pin. Cover any unused portion with a cloth or plastic wrap until needed. Roll the pieces of dough through a pasta machine, starting with the thickest setting and working to the thinnest, until each sheet is ⅛ inch thick. (Alternatively, roll out the dough using a rolling pin.)

Roll the sheets through a fettuccine-cutter attachment or use a knife to cut into ½-inch-wide ribbons.

Lobster mushroom ragout Heat oil in a heavy-bottomed frying pan over medium heat. Add onion and sauté for 5 to 7 minutes, until translucent. Season with a little salt. Increase heat to medium-high and add red pepper. Season again with salt and cook for another 20 minutes, until onions and peppers are caramelized and dark golden brown.

Add vinegar and cook for another 10 to 15 minutes, until reduce by three-quarters. Pour in wine and cook for another 10 minutes, until reduced by half.

In a separate frying pan over high heat, dry-sear mushrooms for 2 to 3 minutes on each side. Transfer mushrooms to pan of onions and peppers. Cook for another 3 to 5 minutes, until thick and saucy. Stir in kelp powder and set aside. Keep warm.

Assembly Bring a large pot of salted water to a boil. Add pasta and cook for 4 to 7 minutes, until 80 percent cooked. Drain pasta, reserving ¼ cup of the pasta water.

Add pasta to the ragout and heat up over medium heat for 2 to 3 minutes, until pasta is coated and sauce has emulsified. Add a little pasta water if it looks dry. Transfer to plates or shallow bowls, garnish with edible flowers (if using) and serve immediately.

Note: Dried kelp can be found online and at many health food stores. If you can't find powdered kelp, you can grind it yourself in a food processor or mortar and pestle. (Canadian Kelp and Cascadia Seaweed are two Island companies that produce it.) You can also substitute powdered dulse.

Quince and Buckwheat Galette

MAKES 8 Quince is an ancient fruit that is enjoying popularity all over the islands. It is similar to a pear or apple, but needs to be cooked to be eaten—and as it is, it turns a beautiful rosy pink colour. At Oxeye, it is a bright flavouring for a rustic galette. If you can't find quince, Blumenthal suggests using heirloom apples or pears.

Toasted buckwheat pastry

¾ cup buckwheat flour

1 cup organic unbleached flour, plus extra for dusting

¼ cup granulated organic sugar

1½ tsp salt

1 cup (2 sticks) cold butter, cubed

3 to 6 Tbsp ice water

Apple jam

4 tart apples, peeled, cored and thinly sliced (4 cups)

1 cup sugar

¼ cup water

Poached quince

2 cups sugar

2 cups water

4 ripe quince, peeled and halved

Assembly

1 egg

1 Tbsp milk or water

Coarse sanding sugar

Toasted buckwheat pastry Preheat oven to 375°F.

Spread buckwheat flour on a baking sheet and toast in oven for 5 minutes, until fragrant and lightly golden. Set aside to cool to room temperature.

In a large mixing bowl, whisk together both flours, sugar and salt.

Using a pastry cutter, cut in cold butter, until it is evenly combined and resembles coarse meal. Add a tablespoon of ice water at a time, until dough comes together. It should clump together, but not be sticky or wet.

On a lightly floured work surface, roll out dough to a ½-inch-thick rectangle and book-fold: with the long side of the dough facing you, fold the edges together to meet in the middle (like a book). Roll it out again to form a ½-inch-thick rectangle, and repeat book-folding and roll-out four more times, until a smooth dough is formed. This adds flaky layers to the pastry. Shape dough into two cylinders, 3 inches wide, then wrap in parchment paper or plastic wrap. Chill in the fridge for at least 2 hours or overnight.

Apple jam Combine apples, sugar and water in a heavy-bottomed saucepan and cook over medium heat for 30 minutes, until a thick jam has formed. Transfer to a food processor and purée until smooth. Set aside to cool.

Poached quince Combine sugar and water in a large heavy-bottomed saucepan. Bring to a simmer over medium heat, stirring, until sugar is fully dissolved, about 5 minutes.

Submerge quince in syrup in one even layer. Bring back up to a simmer over medium heat and cook for 45 minutes to 1 hour, until just soft and yielding. Be sure not to overcook. Set aside to cool. (If you are using apples or pears, this will take as little as 10 minutes, depending on the ripeness of your fruit.)

Using a melon baller or small spoon, scoop out the core and any bits of stem. Slice quince into slices ¼ inch thick.

Assembly Preheat oven to 375°F. Line baking sheet(s) with parchment paper.

Divide pastry dough into 8 equal portions. Roll each dough portion into a circle, 5 to 6 inches in diameter. Spread jam on top, leaving an inch around the perimeter. Arrange sliced quince in a shingled pattern on top of jam, maintaining the circular shape. Fold in and crimp the dough edges to contain the fruit and jam. Place galettes onto prepared baking sheet(s). Refrigerate for 30 minutes.

In a small bowl, combine egg and milk (or water). Brush pastry with egg wash and sprinkle with coarse sugar. Bake for 20 to 30 minutes, until dark golden brown.

PICNIC CHARCUTERIE

Tina Windsor

Tina Windsor isn't quite sure how she ended up as a charcutier in Tofino. "I sort of got conned into starting a business and it's been going almost seven years," she says with a laugh. Then again, you could say her life path was always going to lead her here.

She'd studied organic agriculture in school, then spent the better part of ten years working on farms and ranches, learning about sustainable animal husbandry, including a full season herding sheep and making cheese in Ontario. Eventually she moved to Victoria, where she worked at Choux Choux Charcuterie for two and a half years, learning everything she could from the butcher and chef. In January 2014, she was in Tofino, finishing a contract. "I started talking to people I know and they said, 'Hey, you know how to make sausages, don't you?'" Five months later, with immense support from family and friends, Windsor opened Picnic.

She assembled a team of mostly women to produce high-quality products using local and seasonal B.C. ingredients. "I've hired as many women as possible because it's a male-dominated industry," she says. "We try to make a space that's safe for all people." They make sausages, terrines, salamis and other cured meats that they sell from their storefront, online and to local hotels and restaurants. They also carry cheeses and preserves and prepare ready-made dishes, making everything from kimchi sausage rolls to ramen broth to tapenade and sauerkraut.

What makes their products stand out is the quality of the ingredients. "We grind almost all of our spices fresh and that has a huge impact on taste," Windsor says. "We prioritize the use of naturally raised B.C. meats as much as possible. Meat that comes from an animal that's been active has a structural integrity that a factory product never does. We stay away from industrial as much as we can."

Chicken Liver Pâté

SERVES 8 TO 10 When Picnic Charcuterie owner Tina Windsor decided to make a traditional French chicken liver pâté, she wanted something even creamier than usual, "so we dropped the egg and added duck fat. The high fat concentration, and lack of egg, make it super spreadable, rich and smooth." She recommends using whole spices and grinding them yourself and notes that the pink curing salt—a common preservative that is used to maintain a bright pink colour—is an optional addition.

Spice mix

1½ tsp black peppercorns

2 Tbsp salt

1½ tsp ground sage

½ tsp ground nutmeg

3 g Prague Powder #1 (pink curing salt) (see Note) (optional)

Chicken liver pâté

1 cup (2 sticks) + 2 Tbsp butter, room temperature (divided)

2 sweet onions (1 lb), thinly sliced

1 lb chicken livers, thawed if frozen

Spice Mix (see here)

5 to 6 cloves garlic, finely chopped

3 bay leaves (preferably fresh)

1 cup white wine

½ lb duck fat, room temperature

Assembly

½ cup clarified butter

Chicken Liver Pâté (see here)

8 to 10 bay or sage leaves

Crostini, fresh baguette or cucumber slices, to serve

Spice mix Toast peppercorns in a dry frying pan over medium-high heat for 3 to 5 minutes, until fragrant. Do not burn. Remove from heat, then transfer to a mortar and pestle and allow to cool.

Grind the pepper into a powder and mix it with the rest of the spices. Using a fine-mesh sieve, sift out any chunks. Set aside.

Chicken liver pâté Melt 2 tablespoons butter in a heavy-bottomed frying pan over medium-high heat, until sizzling. Add onions and stir to coat. Reduce heat to medium-low and sauté for 20 to 30 minutes, until caramelized.

Meanwhile, rinse chicken livers in a colander under cool running water until water runs clear. Allow to drip dry.

Add spice mix, garlic and bay leaves to the caramelized onions and cook for 1 to 2 minutes, until fragrant. Stir in chicken livers and cook until warmed through. Pour in wine and simmer for 15 to 20 minutes, until livers are cooked through and reach an internal temperature of 165°F and wine has reduced almost entirely. Discard bay leaves. Set aside to cool to room temperature.

Transfer contents to a deep bowl and, using an immersion blender, pulse to blend. (Alternatively, use a food processor.) Add a chunk of the remaining 1 cup (2 sticks) butter, allowing the piece to dissolve and emulsify. Repeat with an equal amount of duck fat. Alternate between butter and duck fat until everything has been incorporated.

Press through a fine-mesh sieve into a clean bowl, using a spatula to encourage it to push through and to separate the pâté from any solids. While still warm, scoop into 8 to 10 3-inch ramekins or 125 mL Mason jars and smooth out tops. Place ramekins on a tray and refrigerate, covered, for 1 hour, until cold and firmly set.

Assembly Warm clarified butter in a small saucepan over very low heat until just barely liquid but not hot.

Remove ramekins of pâté from fridge. Gently press a bay (or sage) leaf into the centre of each, lying flat. Pour a ¼-inch layer of clarified butter overtop, quickly and gently tilting the ramekin to spread out the butter. (Butter will set quickly on the cold pâté.) The butter does not need to completely cover the leaf, but it should cover the entire surface of the pâté. Once the butter sets, serve with crostini, fresh baguette or cucumber slices.

Note: Leftover pâté can be stored in the fridge for up to 5 days, or 10 days if the curing salt was used. It can also be frozen for up to a year and thawed in the fridge before serving.

Note: Prague Powder #1, also known as pink curing salt, is a curing mixture, a preservative used in some short-cured meat products such as sausages, corned beef, pâtés and terrines. It's mostly table salt, with a small percentage of sodium nitrite, and is often tinted pink so it won't be confused with regular salt. It can be purchased online or at specialty grocers.

Cotechino with Lentils

SERVES 4 This is Picnic Charcuterie's version of a traditional northern Italian New Year's Day meal, "a simple but richly flavoured one-pot recipe." If you don't want to make the sausage from scratch, you can find cotechino ready-made at many artisan delis and butcher shops. But if you are making the sausage at home, you will need: a meat grinder, a sausage stuffer, collagen casings, a crimper and sausage twine, as well as a sausage pricker or fine-tipped knife. This recipe makes two short sausages so they will fit lying flat across the bottom of your pot. The pink curing salt is optional, but charcutier Tina Windsor recommends it because it helps the sausage meat hold together. Pork skin is key to a proper cotechino, and can be purchased from a quality butcher.

Cotechino spice mix

1 tsp coriander seeds
½ tsp black peppercorns
½ tsp white peppercorns
Pinch of celery seeds
1½ tsp salt
½ tsp ground ginger
¼ tsp ground allspice
⅛ tsp ground cinnamon
⅛ tsp ground nutmeg
1.5 g Prague Powder #1
   (pink curing salt)
   (see Note, page 126)
   (optional)

Cotechino sausage

2 (2½ x 12-inch) pre-tied
   collagen casings (see Note)
1 lb pork leg meat
4 oz pork skin
Cotechino Spice Mix
   (see here)
½ cup cold water

Cotechino spice mix Toast coriander seeds, peppercorns and celery seeds in a dry frying pan over medium-high heat for 3 to 5 minutes, until fragrant. Do not burn. Remove from heat and set aside to cool.

Using a mortar and pestle, grind the blend to a powder. Use a fine-mesh sieve to sift out any chunks. Combine with remaining ingredients and set aside.

Cotechino sausage Submerge sausage casings in lukewarm water and soak for at least 30 minutes.

Chill the grinding equipment. When it is cool to the touch, grind the meat and skin separately, using a small ¼-inch plate.

In a large non-reactive bowl, mix together meat, skin and spice mix until fully combined. Add ½ cup water and mix well. Load the meat into the sausage stuffer and thread a casing onto the nozzle. Fill the casing tightly, leaving 3 inches empty at the top end to tie off. Repeat with the second casing.

Hold the sausages, open-end up, and twist the casing ends tightly, ensuring there are no large air pockets. Crimp (or tie) the end. Carefully check sausage for air pockets, releasing any by gently pricking the casing with a sausage pricker or fine-tipped knife. Refrigerate until needed. (Uncooked sausage can be stored in the fridge for up to 3 days. The longer you let it sit, the tangier it'll be.)

Note: Instead of collagen casing, you can use natural beef middles. However, they have a much stronger flavour and inconsistent diameter. Also, the casing often adheres to the meat when cooked, making the final product less attractive once peeled.

Cotechino with lentils Place sausage in a single layer in a Dutch oven or large saucepan. Add enough water to just cover the sausage. Cover and bring to a gentle boil. Add lentils, cover almost completely with water, and simmer for 40 to 45 minutes, using 2 spoons to turn sausage frequently to prevent it from sticking to the bottom. Cook until sausage reaches an internal temperature of 155°F. (When checking the temperature, insert thermometer at a low angle and slowly remove it, so that the pressurized sausage juices don't geyser over your stovetop.)

Meanwhile, melt 2 tablespoons butter in a heavy-bottomed frying pan over medium-high heat, until sizzling. Reduce heat to medium-low, then add onion and sauté for 3 to 5 minutes, until translucent. Add carrots and celeriac (or celery) and sauté for another 5 minutes, until lightly browned. Set aside.

Leaving the sausages in the pot, use a knife to carefully make a shallow slit lengthwise along the sausage casings (do not cut the meat), below the water-line, to release the juices into what is now a beautiful broth. Transfer the 2 pieces of sausage to a grooved cutting board (to catch any juices), brushing any clingy lentils back into the pot. Allow sausage to cool slightly.

Add sautéed vegetables to the pot and simmer over medium-low for 10 to 15 minutes, until vegetables are fully tender and remaining liquid has cooked off. If lentils are still chewy, add enough water to cover and bring to a boil. Reduce to a simmer and cook for another 5 to 10 minutes, until lentils are soft and the liquid has again cooked off. Season with salt.

When sausage is cool enough to handle, remove sausage casings and discard. Cut sausage into ¼-inch rounds. Pour any juices into the pot of lentils.

Heat the remaining 2 tablespoons of butter in a large frying pan over medium-high heat, until sizzling. Working in batches, add sausage rounds in a single layer and cook for 3 to 5 minutes until browned. Flip and cook for another 3 to 5 minutes. Transfer sausage to a plate, then repeat with remaining sausage.

Transfer lentils to 4 shallow bowls, then add sausage. Finish with pepper and parsley, plus grated truffle or a few drops truffle oil (if using).

Cotechino with lentils

1½ lbs store-bought or homemade Cotechino Sausage (see here)

1 cup beluga or Puy lentils

¼ cup (½ stick) butter (divided), plus extra if needed

½ large sweet onion, diced into ½-inch cubes

4 carrots, peeled and diced into ½-inch cubes

1 small celeriac (celery root), peeled, or 2 large stalks celery, cut into ½-inch pieces

Salt and black pepper, to taste

Finely chopped Italian parsley, to taste

Fresh black truffle, grated, or truffle oil (optional)

PLUVIO RESTAURANT + ROOMS

Warren Barr and Lily Verney-Downey

A pluviophile is someone who loves the rain and there's certainly plenty of the wet stuff here on Vancouver Island's west coast. There's plenty of love, too—for food, for community and for each other.

Warren Barr and Lily Verney-Downey met while they were both in the kitchen at the Wickaninnish Inn in Tofino. "Even before Lily and I got together, we had the same idea of what we wanted to do: to be somewhere a little smaller with a few rooms," Barr says. "We met and went, 'That's my dream,'" says Verney-Downey. Barr echoes: "And that's my dream, too."

They had plenty of experience to build on. "Working at the Wick is like going to hospitality university. The experience we gained there was all leading to this project," says Barr, who was executive chef at the inn for six years before opening Pluvio. The couple began looking for a property to make their move. In 2018, they heard that chef Richard Norwood, owner of local favourite Norwoods, just up the road in Ucluelet, was thinking of retiring, and both the restaurant and the land it was on were coming up for sale. This was the opportunity they were looking for and in 2019 they opened Pluvio.

The property isn't huge but has enough room for the thirty-two-seat restaurant, plus a four-room, art-filled boutique hotel they added, and "a tiny forest at the back where I just found chanterelles and porcinis," Barr says. He's continuing to cook the same high-level food he made at the Wick but edited slightly for a more casual crowd. "We try to make food that speaks to where we are, which includes taking influences from the ocean, the land and from Canada's diverse cultures. In Ukee, there are no beaches, it's gnarly, and my food reflects that," Barr says. Adds Verney-Downey: "Warren has spent his whole career working on a Canadian food identity. We want to deliver that elevated restaurant experience, but with it being accessible and friendly, where people just want to hang out. Fun dining, not fine dining."

It's clearly a winning formula: in 2019, Pluvio was ranked #4 on the *enRoute* list of best new

restaurants, and suddenly, tiny Ukee was on the foodie map.

"The local support has been incredible," Verney-Downey says. "We didn't know what to expect, taking on a restaurant that was really loved and changing it, but Ucluelet welcomed us with open arms and we felt at home right away."

Gourmet Granola

MAKES 8 CUPS Mornings at Pluvio mean fresh-baked goods and this wholesome made-from-scratch granola. If you like, serve it with yogurt and fresh fruit.

1¼ cups quinoa

2½ cups water

4 cups canola oil, for deep-frying

⅓ cup wild rice

½ cup sunflower seeds

½ cup pumpkin seeds

6 cups large flake oats

1½ cups raw sugar

1 cup strong English breakfast tea

½ cup canola oil

1 tsp salt

1 tsp vanilla paste or extract

1 cup raisins, roughly chopped

1 cup dried cranberries, roughly chopped

Preheat oven to 350°F.

In a small saucepan, combine quinoa and water and bring to a boil. Reduce heat to medium-low, cover and cook for 10 minutes, until cooked through. Drain. Dry overnight using a dehydrator or in an oven set at 170°F for 6 hours.

Pour the 4 cups of oil in a deep fryer or deep saucepan and heat to a temperature of 350°F. Working in batches, carefully lower quinoa into oil, taking care not to splash hot oil. Deep-fry for a few seconds, until puffed. Using a mesh scoop, transfer quinoa to a paper towel–lined plate. Repeat with remaining quinoa.

Increase oil temperature to 400°F. Carefully lower wild rice into the hot oil and deep-fry for a few seconds until puffed. Using a mesh scoop, transfer wild rice to a paper towel–lined plate.

Line a baking sheet with parchment paper. Spread out sunflower seeds and pumpkin seeds on it and toast in the oven for 10 minutes, until golden and fragrant. Remove from oven and reduce oven to 250°F.

Add quinoa, wild rice and oats to the baking sheet with the seeds. When the oven is to temperature, bake for 1 to 2 hours, until dry and aromatic. Transfer mixture to a large bowl. Reduce oven heat to 200°F.

In a small saucepan, combine sugar, tea, the ½ cup oil, salt and vanilla and bring to a simmer over medium heat. Cook for 15 minutes, until reduced by half.

Pour the syrup into the granola mixture and stir until well mixed and clumpy. Spread granola across 2 baking sheets and bake for 1 hour, until sticky and almost dry. Remove from oven and set aside to cool. Transfer to a large bowl and mix in raisins and cranberries. (Granola can be stored in an airtight container for several weeks.)

Truffle Tuna Tartare

SERVES 4 Albacore tuna is one of the most sustainable fish on this coast, and it stars in this luxurious, complexly textured dish. Island truffles are available October through December from Below the Nut Farm, but if you can't get your hands on them, a few aromatic drops of truffle oil will also work nicely.

Rice crisps

½ cup Thai sweet rice (glutinous rice)

3 cups water

1 tsp activated charcoal powder

4 cups canola oil

Salt, to taste

Tuna tartare

30 dried shiitake mushrooms (divided)

1 cup canola oil

½ cup sugar

1 cup rice vinegar (divided)

¼ cup soy sauce

½ cup water

1 (14-oz) sashimi-grade albacore tuna loin, slightly thawed if frozen

½ tsp salt, or to taste

Assembly

Juice of ½ lime

Truffle oil, to taste

½ shallot, finely chopped

5 chives, thinly sliced

4 to 6 radishes, thinly sliced on a mandoline

Microgreens, for garnish

Edible flowers, for garnish

Fresh truffle (preferably from Below the Nut Farm), grated

Rice crisps Place the rice, water and charcoal powder in a small saucepan. Bring to a boil, then cover and reduce heat to medium-low. Cook for 20 minutes, until rice is overcooked. Set aside to cool to room temperature.

Transfer rice to a food processor or blender and blend until smooth.

Cut a sheet of parchment paper to fit into a dehydrator (or alternatively, a baking sheet that can be put in the oven.) Spread paste ⅛-inch thick onto prepared parchment and leave in the dehydrator overnight, until very dry and brittle. (Alternatively, dry in an oven set at 170°F for 6 hours.) Break into 4 randomly shaped pieces. Note that you may have more than you need.

Pour oil into a medium saucepan, to 2 inches deep, and heat to a temperature of 375°F. Carefully lower one dried rice crisp into the pan, taking care not to splash hot oil. Deep-fry for 5 to 10 seconds, until it puffs up into a crunchy, wild-looking cracker. If it doesn't, remove the crisp, heat the oil a bit more and try again. Set aside on a paper towel–lined plate and season with a bit of salt. Repeat with the remaining crisps.

Tuna tartare In a blender, combine 15 shiitakes and oil. Blend on high speed until the outside of the jug is slightly warm to the touch. Pour oil into a bowl and set aside. It will have a pleasant mushroom flavour and aroma.

Chop remaining shiitakes into a ¼-inch dice. Set aside.

In a small saucepan, combine sugar and ½ cup rice vinegar and bring to a simmer over medium heat. Cook for 10 to 15 minutes, stirring occasionally, until golden caramel.

Meanwhile, in another small saucepan over medium heat, combine remaining ½ cup vinegar with soy sauce and water and bring to a simmer.

To avoid burning yourself, slowly and carefully drizzle the warm soy mixture into the caramel mixture. Add chopped shiitakes and cook for 10 minutes over medium heat, until slightly syrupy. Set aside and allow to cool to room temperature. You will have about 1 cup shiitake-soy caramel in total.

Cut tuna into ½-inch cubes and transfer into a bowl. Season with salt and pour over with enough shiitake oil to coat each cube when mixed. Add a little extra for good luck. Cover and refrigerate until needed. (Any leftover shiitake oil can be reserved for later use—it makes a great foundation for salad dressings.)

Assembly Add half of the shiitake-soy caramel to the marinated tuna and gently toss. Add more mushrooms, if desired. (The caramel is rich so taste as you go to decide how much you want to use—you may not want to use it all.) Season with a few drops of lime juice and truffle oil, and some shallots and chives. Adjust seasoning to taste.

Lay a rice crisp on each plate. Place a large spoonful of dressed tuna in the centre. Gently press down tuna to be slightly flat. Fan radishes over each pile of tuna to resemble fish scales. Garnish with microgreens and edible flowers and finish with grated truffle. Serve immediately.

POETS COVE RESORT & SPA

Jesse Francis

From the ferry, it's a much longer drive than you'd think it could be—past bustling Driftwood Centre and bucolic farms, across the bridge that replaced the isthmus that once connected North and South Pender Island, along winding roads through an enchanted forest—before you arrive at the luxurious Poets Cove Resort and go ahhhh.

"There's a lot of magical things here," says Jesse Francis, who has been the chef at the resort since 2015. Originally from Alberta, he arrived after nearly a dozen years of working at the Fairmont Jasper Park Lodge and sees a lot of similarity between the two. Mind you, Poets Cove is newer, built in 2004 on the site of a much more rustic resort that dated back to 1959. And it has a marina with a customs office and an aerodrome.

Poets Cove boasts two dining outlets, the fine-dining Aurora Restaurant and casual Syrens Bistro & Lounge, as well as the grab-and-go Moorings Market. (The marina provides some of their best customers, of course.) And Francis is working hard to put the resort—and by extension, Pender—on the map. "We have a mission to elevate the marina and turn it into a culinary destination," he says.

That starts with sourcing exceptional local ingredients. "Obviously, looking at the ocean every day, you need to have seafood on the menu," he says. "Plus rosemary and blackberries have been really inspiring for me because we have a lot of both on the property. There's also some really good lamb on Pender." Francis also works closely with Raven Rock Farm, a small certified organic farm located on a south-facing hillside on the island, to acquire his fresh produce. And Francis explores his creativity at Poets Cove by hosting specialty wine-pairing dinners featuring local wines from Sea Star Estate Farm and Vineyards.

He adds: "I like to cook with a bit of a twist. It's important to make food fun and interesting for people at the same time."

Black and Blue Salad

SERVES 4 In chef Jesse Francis's take on the classic salad, the "black" comes from the blackberries that grow wild all over Pender and the other Gulf Islands. A brown butter vinaigrette and bacon brittle add warmth and texture to this bright side dish. Note that you will need a candy thermometer when making the brittle.

Brown butter vinaigrette

1 cup (2 sticks) butter
1 shallot, finely chopped
⅓ cup sherry vinegar
1 tsp chopped rosemary

Bacon brittle

12 slices thick-cut bacon, diced
1 cup sugar
½ cup + 2 Tbsp light corn syrup
½ cup + 2 Tbsp water + ½ tsp (divided)
2 tsp butter
1 tsp baking soda
½ tsp vanilla extract

Assembly

4 cups mixed greens (8 oz)
Brown Butter Vinaigrette (see here)
4 oz smoked blue cheese
2 cups blackberries
Bacon Brittle (see here)

Brown butter vinaigrette Melt butter in a small saucepan over medium heat and whisk for 5 to 7 minutes, until nutty and caramel in colour.

Place shallot in a large bowl and pour in warm brown butter, which will bubble and foam up. Whisk in vinegar and rosemary, then set aside.

Bacon brittle Line 2 baking sheets with silicone mats or aluminum foil.

In a large frying pan, fry bacon for 4 to 7 minutes over medium-low heat, stirring occasionally, until crisp. Use a slotted spoon to transfer bacon to a paper towel–lined plate. You will need ¾ cup of the finished lardons.

In a heavy-bottomed saucepan, combine sugar, corn syrup and ½ cup + 2 Tbsp water and bring to a boil. Reduce heat to medium and simmer until temperature reads 240°F on a candy thermometer.

Add butter and stir constantly, until temperature reads 300°F (the hard-crack stage).

Working quickly and carefully, stir in bacon, baking soda, vanilla and ½ tsp water. Immediately pour mixture onto the prepared baking sheets and spread out using a silicone spatula. Set aside to cool and harden.

Transfer brittle to a food processor and pulse until just crumbled.

Assembly In a large bowl, toss mixed greens with 2 to 3 tablespoons vinaigrette. Add more vinaigrette to taste. Divide among 4 plates or place in a large serving bowl. Dress with blue cheese, blackberries and bacon brittle, then serve.

Oyster Tacos

SERVES 4 The oysters that come from the pristine waters off Vancouver Island are among the best in the world. Here, they're pan-seared, then tucked into tacos. If you don't feel like shucking them yourself, look for containers of pre-shucked Fanny Bay oysters in your fishmonger's case.

Avocado-lime cream
1 avocado, coarsely chopped
¼ cup sour cream
Juice of 1 lime
Salt and black pepper, to taste

Corn pico de gallo
1 ear of corn, shucked
Salt and black pepper, to taste
2 tsp vegetable oil, plus extra if needed
1 Roma tomato, finely chopped
1 jalapeño pepper, finely chopped
½ small red onion, finely chopped
¼ cup chopped cilantro
Juice of 1 lime

Pan-seared oysters
1 cup cornmeal
1 tsp Old Bay seasoning
8 fresh medium-large oysters, shucked
1 egg, beaten
¼ cup canola oil
1 Tbsp olive oil

Assembly
8 (6-inch) corn or flour tortillas
2 radishes, thinly sliced
Chopped cilantro, to taste

Avocado-lime cream Place all ingredients in a blender or food processor and blend until smooth. Adjust seasoning to taste.

Corn pico de gallo Preheat grill over high heat.

Rub corn with salt and pepper and enough oil to lightly coat. Add corn to grill and grill on all sides, for 5 to 10 minutes total, until some of it is charred. Set aside to cool.

Shave kernels off the cob. Transfer corn to a bowl, add remaining ingredients and mix together. Adjust seasoning to taste.

Pan-seared oysters In a small bowl, combine cornmeal and Old Bay seasoning and mix well.

Pat oysters dry. Dip them in beaten egg, shaking off any excess, then roll in the cornmeal mixture and ensure they are well coated. Transfer to a plate and refrigerate for 5 minutes to allow coating to stick to oysters.

Heat the oils together in a frying pan over medium-high heat. Fry oysters for 1 to 2 minutes on each side, until golden brown. Transfer to a paper towel–lined plate.

Assembly Warm tortillas in oven or on grill.

Place seared oysters on warm tortillas. Add corn pico di gallo, then drizzle avocado-lime cream overtop. Garnish with radishes and cilantro and serve immediately.

SALTCHUCK PIE COMPANY

Nick Crooks

When Nick Crooks moved to Victoria twenty years ago from his native New Zealand by way of Australia, there was just one thing he missed. Well, two. "Meat pies and Asian street food," says Crooks.

Although he'd been a chef at top restaurants in Australia, he decided to start a pie bakery. When that fell through, he opened a food truck, serving "the tasty things I ate while I was backpacking around the world." It eventually became the Noodle Box, which he sold in 2013. Then Crooks went travelling again. This time when he returned to Victoria, he decided to follow his first dream. "The pies are something I grew up with as a Kiwi," he says. "Pies are everywhere. Every corner store and gas station."

Meat pies from Down Under are different from British and North American ones. The secret is the laminated, puff-style pastry, which makes for a crisp, flaky, buttery crust. Aside from that, Crooks says, "A pie is basically a stew with a pastry shell."

And that gives him endless flexibility to try new things. He's made a turkey dinner pie with a stuffing cap, chicken paneer pie and kangaroo pie with truffled mushrooms. He serves four different breakfast pies a day, including a full English and a vegetarian option. "We do a steak with a caramelized onion and blue cheese and I could eat that every day," he says. "It's great because I get to play around and order cool things."

And now that he has access to the pies he loves, he figures Victoria is a perfect city. "It's a good place for me to be creative," he says. "It's lovely because I'm five years in and people are still bringing me ideas."

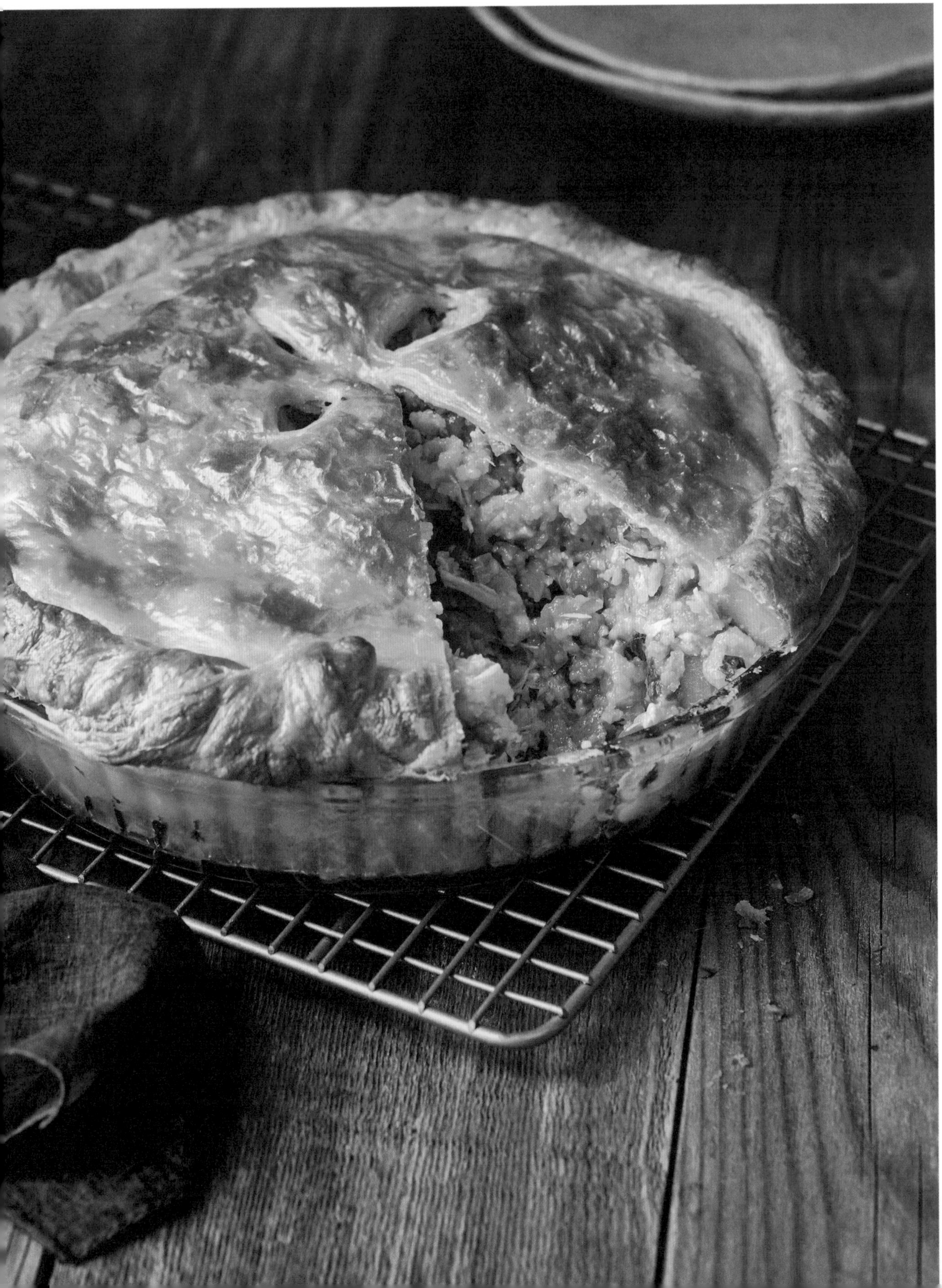

Farmhouse Rabbit Pie, p. 140

Farmhouse Rabbit Pie

SERVES 6 TO 8 For this centrepiece pie, Saltchuck Pie Company founder Nick Crooks loves rabbit meat, which he says "is wonderfully lean and flavourful." However, if your butcher doesn't carry it, a free-range chicken makes a good substitute. This recipe is best cooked over two days, Crooks advises, and a 10-inch fluted ceramic pie dish will give you the best results.

2 Tbsp canola oil

1 rabbit, cut into 6 pieces (ask your butcher)

Flour, for dredging and dusting

Salt and black pepper, to taste

2 sprigs rosemary

2 sprigs thyme

1 bay leaf

6 to 8 cups water

¼ cup (½ stick) butter, plus extra for greasing

1 onion, chopped

1 leek, white and light green parts only, halved lengthwise and sliced

2 carrots, chopped

3 stalks celery, chopped

4 to 6 cloves garlic, crushed

1 cup dry white wine

2 Tbsp soy sauce

1 Tbsp tomato paste

1 cup cornstarch

1 cup water

½ bunch Italian parsley, chopped

1 cup green peas

1 cup heavy (36%) cream

2 lbs store-bought all-butter puff pastry (roughly 2 boxes)

1 egg, beaten

Preheat oven to 350°F.

Heat oil in a frying pan over medium heat. Dredge rabbit in flour, then add to pan and pan-fry for 5 to 10 minutes on each side until evenly brown.

Transfer rabbit to a Dutch oven, then add salt, pepper, herbs and enough water to cover (at least 6 cups). Place in the oven and cook for 1½ hours, until meat falls easily from the bone. Remove rabbit and set aside to cool.

Strain braising liquid and reserve. Carefully remove meat and discard bones. Roughly chop.

Melt butter in a heavy saucepan over medium heat. Add onion, leek, carrots, celery and garlic and sauté for 10 minutes, until softened. Add wine, soy sauce, tomato paste and 4 cups of braising liquid (reserving the rest) and bring to a boil. Reduce heat to medium-low and simmer, uncovered, for 30 minutes.

In a small bowl, combine cornstarch and 1 cup water. Whisk in ½ cup of the cornstarch slurry into the mixture and simmer until it has a rich and thick gravy-like consistency. Add more braising liquid if it's too thick or more slurry if it's too thin. Add rabbit, parsley, peas and cream and stir well. Taste and adjust seasoning. Set aside to cool.

Preheat oven to 400°F. Grease a deep 10-inch pie pan.

On a lightly floured work surface, roll puff pastry to an ⅛ inch thickness. Cut one 11-inch piece of pastry for the top. Cut out another 13-inch piece of pastry for the bottom.

Line pie pan with the pastry bottom. Add the filling, then brush a little of the whisked egg around the join. Carefully lay the other piece of pastry overtop. Crimp edges to seal, then pierce the top with a few 1-inch vents. (Use any excess filling and pastry to make small pies for the freezer.)

Brush the top of the pastry with the remaining egg wash and bake for 25 to 30 minutes, until the pie is crisp and golden brown. Let rest for 10 to 15 minutes, then serve.

Blackberry-Vanilla Lamingtons

MAKES 24 INDIVIDUAL CAKES Lamingtons are delightful individual cakes popular in Australia and New Zealand, where Saltchuck Pie Company founder Nick Crooks comes from. They are perfect for afternoon tea or a summer picnic, so brew a pot of Earl Grey tea, he suggests, and lay out your best doilies!

Sponge cake

5 eggs
1 cup sugar
1½ cups flour
1 tsp baking powder
¼ tsp salt
6 Tbsp (¾ stick) butter, melted
½ cup milk
1 tsp vanilla extract

Blackberry icing

½ cup milk
½ cup blackberry jam
2 Tbsp butter
2 cups icing sugar

Assembly

Sponge Cake (see here)
½ cup blackberry jam
Blackberry Icing (see here)
2 cups desiccated coconut
2 cups whipping (33%) cream
2 tsp vanilla extract
2 Tbsp icing sugar

Sponge cake Preheat oven to 350°F. Line an 8 x 12-inch baking pan with parchment paper.

In a stand mixer fitted with a paddle attachment, combine eggs and sugar and beat for 7 minutes, until thick and pale.

In a separate bowl, combine flour, baking powder and salt.

In a third bowl, combine butter, milk and vanilla.

Add a third of the flour mixture to the egg mixture and mix on low speed. Add half of the milk mixture and mix again on low speed. Continue to alternate the dry and wet ingredients and beat until no trace of flour remains. Pour batter into prepared baking pan and bake for 15 to 18 minutes, until lightly browned and a toothpick inserted into the centre comes out clean. Set aside to cool.

Blackberry icing Combine milk, jam and butter in a small saucepan and bring to a simmer over medium heat. Stir in icing sugar and mix well. Transfer to a shallow bowl and set aside until needed.

Assembly Slice sponge cake in half horizontally.

Spread blackberry jam on the base and top it with the other half of the cake. Cut cake into 2-inch squares.

Spread coconut out on a plate. Using 2 forks, dip and roll the individual cakes in the blackberry icing, covering them lightly on all sides, then roll cakes in coconut. Place on a rack on top of a baking sheet. Refrigerate for 30 minutes.

In a large bowl, combine cream, vanilla and icing sugar and whip until soft peaks form.

Serve lamingtons with vanilla whipped cream.

SALTSPRING KITCHEN CO.

Melanie Mulherin

Melanie Mulherin credits two strong women for her success as a culinary entrepreneur. The first was her single mom, who raised her in Kelowna. "My mom was creative and scrappy and always found a way to put food on the table," Mulherin says. "It was incredible what she did with very limited resources."

Just as influential was her mother-in-law, who taught Mulherin the art of preserving during the eight years she and her chef husband ran a restaurant in northern B.C. "Our restaurant is where we started our spicy tomato preserve, which is one of our bestsellers today," she says.

Eventually the couple relocated to Salt Spring Island and, one day in 2012, Mulherin made some preserves in her kitchen and took them to the island's lively farmers' market to see how they'd be received.

The next time she set up her stall, David Wood, the founder of the famous Salt Spring Island Cheese Company, told her, "These preserves would be perfect in our farm shop." He urged her to treat her preserves like a business, so she set about creating a brand identity. "Salt Spring Cheese is still one of our best customers today," she says. "Connecting with Salt Spring Island Cheese really helped me hone in on what I wanted to do."

Today she produces a full line of savoury, spicy and sweet preserves, including the popular seeded Charcuterie Mustard that "we liken to mustard caviar," the Candied Jalapeños burger relish, several hot sauces and the versatile Onion & Thyme Savoury Spread that is used in the recipe on page 143.

And she's not making jam in her home kitchen anymore. "We ended up building a little kitchen above our garage. It was adorable, but I couldn't have anyone else in there with me," she says She's since moved into a custom-built preserving kitchen and has future plans for expansion.

One-Pan Chicken and Mushrooms with Onion-Thyme Cream Sauce

SERVES 4 "This recipe was inspired by the beautiful chanterelles my neighbour had just gifted me and the abundance of apple products going through my kitchen," says Saltspring Kitchen founder Melanie Mulherin. Her onion and thyme spread is a savoury blend of onions, apples, balsamic and apple cider vinegars and is a great shortcut for making dinner. Serve this dish with rice, egg noodles or mashed potatoes and a green salad.

2 Tbsp canola oil

8 bone-in, skin-on chicken thighs

Sea salt and black pepper, to taste

1 shallot, finely chopped

2 cloves garlic, finely chopped

3 cups mixed mushrooms, such as cremini and chanterelles, sliced

1 Tbsp thyme leaves

Pinch of crushed red pepper

¾ cup hard apple cider, white wine or chicken stock

1 (270-mL) jar Saltspring Kitchen Co. Onion & Thyme Savoury Spread

1 cup whipping (33%) cream

Heat oil in a large frying pan over medium-high heat. Season chicken with salt and pepper, then add to the pan, skin-side down. Fry for 10 minutes, until skin is crisp and brown. Flip and cook for another 10 to 15 minutes, until cooked through. Transfer chicken to a plate and set aside.

Add shallot and garlic to the pan. Sauté for 2 to 3 minutes, then add mushrooms, thyme and crushed red pepper. Season with salt and pepper. Reduce heat to medium and cook for 10 to 15 minutes, until mixture is nearly dry.

Pour in cider (or wine or stock) and cook off for 10 minutes. Stir in the onion and thyme spread and the cream. Add chicken to the pan and simmer until heated through.

Autumn Crush Bourbon Cocktail

SERVES 1 Fruit spreads aren't just for toast; they also make a terrific sweetener in cocktails. Here Saltspring Kitchen founder Melanie Mulherin adds an apricot and pink peppercorn spread to bourbon for a flavour that is both deep and zippy.

1½ oz bourbon

1½ oz sweet apple cider

¼ oz lemon juice

1 heaping tsp Saltspring Kitchen Co. Sparkling Apricot & Pink Peppercorn Fruit Spread

6 dashes bitters (preferably Mister Bitters Fig & Cinnamon)

Apple chip, for garnish

Cinnamon, for garnish

Fill a cocktail shaker with ice. Add all ingredients except the garnishes and shake for 20 seconds. Double strain into a cocktail glass. Garnish with apple chip and a dash of cinnamon.

SEA BREEZE LODGE

The Bishop Family

It's coming up on half a century since Brian and Gail Bishop bought this property on Hornby Island, one of the northernmost of the Gulf Islands. Before 1972, it was the Sea Breeze Guest Farm, a place where guests would help milk the cows and collect the eggs. Since then, the Bishop family has developed the property into a large waterfront resort and restaurant where guests can sit back and let the hosts do the work.

In the early years, Gail did all the cooking herself and focused on providing hearty, home-cooked meals for their guests. As the business grew, Brian and Gail's sons, Jeffrey and Stephen, took over the daily operations of the business with their families. Gail passed her culinary knowledge (and a well-used Sea Breeze cookbook) on to Suzie Bishop, the wife of Stephen Bishop, the middle of Brian and Gail's three sons. "There are three generations who work here today," Stephen says. "My dad's on the lawnmower right now!"

The family-friendly lodge is open year-round and has a loyal clientele, some of whom have been coming back for forty years. Meals are casual and feature local products such as seafood, garden-fresh produce and libations from the island's brewery and wineries.

"The restaurant has changed over the years," says Carlyn, Stephen's daughter. For one thing, although Suzie and Gail are still around to offer advice in the kitchen, the restaurant now has a head chef. For another, in addition to the traditional buffet service, they now offer seasonally inspired a la carte menus. "Everything is a bit more modern. We've always had different cuisines, like our Thai buffet or Mexican buffet. Now we're bringing all those influences into our dishes. But one thing that has remained consistent is the comforting, family-style food."

After all, Carlyn says, "Our family history is an important part of the business." Guests, old and new, appreciate the comfort of the home-style cooking and family atmosphere, no matter who is in the kitchen.

Salmon Chowder and Irish Soda Bread, p. 148

Salmon Chowder

SERVES 4 TO 6 The waters around Hornby Island produce exceptional seafood, including salmon, which stars in this rich, savoury chowder from Sea Breeze Lodge co-owner Suzie Bishop. Chowder is perhaps *the* essential food on the islands—it is typically creamy (except for the tomato-based ones served on BC Ferries) and packed with clams, mussels, scallops, oysters and/or fin fish.

⅓ cup pickling spice

2 Tbsp butter

1 Tbsp olive oil

2 onions, chopped

6 stalks celery, chopped

Salt and black pepper, to taste

4 large potatoes, peeled and cut into ½-inch cubes

3 cloves garlic, finely chopped

1 Tbsp chopped dill

4 cups seafood stock

2 cups whipping (33%) cream

⅓ cup ketchup

1½ lbs salmon, skinned, deboned and cubed

Irish Soda Bread, to serve (optional) (page 149)

Put pickling spice in a cheesecloth and tie tightly.

Heat butter and oil in a large saucepan over medium heat. Add onions and celery and sauté for 5 minutes, until softened. Season with salt and pepper. Add potatoes, garlic and dill and sauté for another 5 minutes.

Add stock and pickling spice bundle. Bring to a boil, then reduce heat to medium-low and simmer for 15 minutes. Stir in cream and ketchup and simmer another 15 minutes. Add salmon and cook for 2 to 3 minutes, until just cooked through. Remove spice bundle.

Serve with Irish soda bread, if desired.

Irish Soda Bread

MAKES 1 LOAF "This soda bread recipe was passed down from the original owner, Evelyn Fowler, to my grandmother, who passed it down to my mother, who has passed it on to our chefs," says Carlyn Bishop. It's the perfect thing to soak up every last drop of creamy deliciousness in a bowl of chowder (page 148).

2½ cups whole wheat flour

1½ cups flour, plus extra for dusting

2 tsp salt

2 tsp baking soda

2 tsp baking powder

½ cup (1 stick) butter

2 cups buttermilk

Preheat oven to 375°F.

In a large stainless steel bowl, combine the dry ingredients. Cut in butter until it resembles coarse crumbs. Make a well in the centre and pour in buttermilk. Mix gently until it just comes together.

Turn out dough onto a lightly floured work surface and knead gently to form a ball. Place on a baking sheet and use a serrated knife to slice through the middle of the ball, almost to the bottom. Bake for 35 to 40 minutes, until golden brown and cooked through.

SHELTER RESTAURANT

Matty Kane

The location is legendary. Back when Tofino was just a rain-soaked hippie village at the end of a logging road, this was the Crab Shack, a smoky, one-room joint where everyone gathered to enjoy one of two menu items: half of a boiled Dungeness crab or a whole one.

Now, though, this is Shelter, a rambling, stylishly rustic hot spot with a popular patio and a cosy fireplace for gathering around on those stormy days. As for the menu, under chef Matty Kane's direction, it's a pretty generous one. "You can have a burger, but if you want to have an elevated dining experience you can do that as well," he says. "We're trying to hit all the notes. It's about the dining experience, the vibe."

Kane himself hails from the other side of the country. "It's a classic East Coast–West Coast story. When I left Newfoundland, the food scene was pretty conservative and there wasn't much going on," he says. "When I came here, it was refreshing—not just to see people cooking fresh and interesting food, but also people who were excited to eat it."

That was in 2007, four years after Shelter opened. Back then there were only a handful of restaurants in Tofino. "It was pretty mellow," Kane says. "You could ride your bike from the middle of town to Chesterman Beach and not see another person." In 2014, things began to change. New restaurants opened; meanwhile, Shelter's owner Jay Gildenhuys led the charge to create both the annual Feast Tofino festival and the Tofino Ucluelet Culinary Guild.

"We get a lot of our produce from the guild. They source the products from the Island, some from the Okanagan," Kane says. That could include the salmon for their "insanely popular" surf bowl, or the halibut he likes to serve with a brothy mushroom purée, for which you can find the recipe on page 152. Other times, he teams up with local farmers and gets them to produce the things he needs for the coming season.

"They get the benefit of guaranteed crop sales, and we get access to great local produce in the quantities we require," he says. "We do what we can when we can."

Leek-Cured Salmon Tostada with Avocado, Crema and Chili Oil

SERVES 2 | Matty Kane, chef at Tofino's Shelter Restaurant, advises that you can use any combination of whole Mexican chilies you like for the chili oil, but to be cautious with really spicy ones, like chipotles and chiles de àrbol. Dried Mexican chilies are available at many well-stocked grocery stores, and it's best to make the oil the day before tackling the rest of this appetizer dish. Or if time is of the essence, you can use a purchased chili oil instead.

1 leek, light and green parts only, cut into chunks

1 cup salt, for leek salt

1 cup well-packed whole dried chilies, such as guajillo, pasilla or morita

1 cup grapeseed oil

½ lb salmon fillet, skin removed

½ cup white vinegar

½ cup water

2½ tsp salt (divided)

2 tsp sugar

3 shallots, thinly sliced

1 small jalapeño pepper, seeded and thinly sliced

½ cup sour cream

2 Tbsp whipping (33%) cream

2 ripe avocados

Juice of 1 lime

4 cups canola or grapeseed oil, for deep-frying

2 (6-inch) corn tortillas

Assembly

2 sprigs of cilantro, leaves only, for garnish

Place leek in a small non-reactive container. Cover with the 1 cup of salt and refrigerate, uncovered, overnight. The salt will remove moisture from the leek and take on its earthy flavour.

Place chilies and the 1 cup of grapeseed oil in a blender and blend on high speed for 3 to 5 minutes. Transfer to a bowl or Mason jar and set aside at room temperature overnight. (Chili oil can be stored in the fridge for up to a month.)

The next day, cut salmon into 3 to 4 pieces and place in a non-reactive container or a resealable bag. Add the leek salt (including the chopped leek pieces) and gently massage it around, until salmon is evenly coated. Refrigerate for 1 hour.

In a small saucepan, combine vinegar, water, 2 tsp salt and sugar and bring to a simmer. Place shallots and jalapeño in a non-reactive heatproof bowl. Pour the simmering liquid in the bowl. Immediately add 2 ice cubes and set aside.

In a small bowl, combine sour cream, whipping cream and ¼ tsp of salt. Spoon crema into a squeeze bottle.

Pit and peel the avocados. Place avocado, lime juice and ¼ tsp of salt in a food processor and pulse until smooth.

Pour the 4 cups of oil into a deep fryer or deep saucepan and heat to a temperature of 350°F. Gently lower in tortillas and deep-fry for 1 minute or until they start to brown and crisp up. Transfer tostadas to a paper towel–lined plate to drain.

Transfer salmon to a colander and rinse under cold running water. Pat dry with a paper towel and cut into ½-inch cubes.

Assembly Spoon avocado purée onto each tostada, spreading it to cover all but the very edge. Arrange a few dots of crema around the tostada and on top of the avocado purée.

Spoon salmon onto the tostadas in a single layer. Place tostadas on plates and, if you wish, use a kitchen torch to char salmon evenly. (It's okay to char the tortilla and the purée a little at this stage.)

Add a few more dots of crema on top, then garnish with shallot and jalapeño pickles, a dot of chili oil and cilantro. Serve immediately.

Pan-Roasted Halibut with Roasted Mushroom Broth and Crispy Potatoes

SERVES 2 Halibut is one of the most valued fin fish on this coast, at once sturdy and delicate. At Shelter, chef Matty Kane serves it with the earthy flavours of mushrooms, potatoes and sesame. Just be super careful not to overcook the fish— it takes only seconds to go from perfect to disappointing.

2 large russet potatoes, skin on

Salt

1 Tbsp sherry vinegar

1 Tbsp shoyu (see Note)

Juice of 1 lemon (divided)

Bunch of large green onions

¼ cup (½ stick) salted butter

8 large cremini mushrooms, thinly sliced

½ cup water, plus extra if needed

4 cups grapeseed oil, for deep-frying

1 Tbsp sesame seeds

¼ tsp toasted sesame oil

2 Tbsp grapeseed oil, plus extra for frying

Black pepper, to taste

2 (8-oz) skinless halibut fillets

Place potatoes in a small saucepan, then cover with water and add a generous amount of salt. Bring to a boil, then reduce heat to medium-low and simmer for 20 minutes. Drain, then set aside to cool. (This can be done well ahead of time.)

In a small bowl, combine vinegar, shoyu and 1 tablespoon lemon juice and mix well. Set aside.

Fill a small bowl with ice and water. Slice onion stalks lengthwise into very thin strips. Place onions in the ice bath and set aside until they curl up.

Heat butter in a medium saucepan over medium heat until it begins to foam. Add mushrooms and pan-roast them, stirring occasionally, until they brown. Add water, cover and reduce heat to low. Cook for 5 minutes.

Transfer mushrooms and liquid to a blender, then add half of the shoyu mixture and blend on high speed until smooth. If the purée is a bit too thick, add a little water as needed. Transfer to a small saucepan and reserve until needed.

Pour the 4 cups of grapeseed oil into a deep fryer or deep saucepan and heat to a temperature of 350°F. Using your fingers, break up potatoes into irregular pieces, slightly larger than bite-sized. Carefully lower potatoes into the fryer (or pan), taking care not to splash hot oil. Deep-fry for 3 to 5 minutes until golden brown. Transfer potatoes to a paper towel–lined plate.

Using a mortar and pestle, grind sesame seeds to a paste. Add the paste to the remaining half of the shoyu mixture, along with the sesame oil and the 2 table-spoons grapeseed oil. Season the sesame vinaigrette with pepper.

Heat enough oil to cover the bottom of a large frying pan over medium-high heat. Season halibut with salt and pepper. Add halibut to pan, then reduce heat to medium-low and pan-sear for 3 to 5 minutes, until golden brown. Turn fillets and cook for another 3 to 5 minutes, spooning pan juices over the halibut to help cook it more evenly. Be careful not to overcook.

Transfer halibut to a wire rack, then drizzle the remaining lemon juice overtop.

Assembly Spoon enough hot mushroom purée into 2 shallow bowls to cover the bottom. Place halibut slightly to the side of the plate.

Season crispy potatoes with salt and pepper, then place next to the fillets. Drain onions, then dress them with half the sesame vinaigrette. Spoon remaining vinaigrette over the halibut and potatoes, garnish fillets with the onions and finish with black pepper. Serve immediately.

Note: Shoyu is the name for Japanese soy sauce, which is made from fermented soy and wheat and is sweeter and lighter than its Chinese counterpart.

SOBO

Lisa Ahier

Before 2003, people came to Tofino for the surf, the fishing and sometimes the protests. Then Lisa Ahier started serving fish tacos and polenta fries from a purple food truck. A few months later, SoBo—for "sophisticated bohemian"—made the top-ten list of *enRoute*'s Best New Restaurants. Now the best reason to visit Tofino is the food.

Ahier learned to cook as a little girl at the Texas truck stop where her mom worked, then studied at the Culinary Institute of America in New York. She returned to Texas to become executive chef at Cibolo Creek Ranch. "My first customer was Mick Jagger. He and Jerry Hall would come to the ranch," she recalls.

From there, the journey brought her and her then-husband to Vancouver Island, where she was wowed by the incredible produce. "Vancouver Island is all about product," she says. She was overwhelmed by the groundbreaking Sooke Harbour House and its owners at the time, Frédérique and Sinclair Philip. "I was so awestruck by what I saw them doing there," she says. "Sinclair was diving for sea urchins and they had all these crazy little vegetables that I'd never heard of growing in the garden. And the customers were willing to gamble on it with them."

She was the opening chef at Long Beach Lodge Resort but wanted to have her own place. And so came about the food truck, which four years later became the bricks-and-mortar restaurant in downtown Tofino, where she still serves her famous margaritas, the salmon chowder that won a major investment on *Dragon's Den* and all the other dishes locals and visitors alike love so much.

"I like the vegetable dishes the best," Ahier says. "I'm so excited right now because we have chanterelle mushrooms and perfect corn and tomatoes," she says. "Things are so good at the moment with the gardens and the farms. When ingredients are this good, you don't need to do all these sauces. It's so vibrant on the palate. I'm losing my mind from all this stuff."

Wild Nettle and Sorrel Soup

SERVES 4 TO 6 Nettles are one of the first signs of spring on Vancouver Island. "They are nature's way of waking us up gently with a healing, cleansing, calcium-rich treat right when we need it most," says SoBo's Lisa Ahier.

Nettles have curative properties that relieve inflammation, which is why Ahier saves the blanching water from this recipe and adds it to her bath. Still, we recommend wearing gloves and long-sleeved shirts when picking nettles to avoid their stinging hairs. If you cannot find wild nettles, they can be replaced by spinach, kale or even chard.

Roast garlic

2 heads garlic
1 to 2 tsp olive oil

Wild nettle and sorrel soup

4 L water
6 Tbsp salt (divided), plus extra to taste
2 lbs wild nettle leaves, stems removed
½ cup olive oil
2 large leeks, white and light green parts only, finely chopped
½ cup finely chopped celery
¼ cup finely chopped garlic
4 cups vegetable stock
1 large Yukon Gold potato, cut into ½-inch cubes
½ cup Roasted Garlic (see here)
¼ cup thyme leaves
2 Tbsp hot sauce (preferably Frank's RedHot)
6 cups sorrel leaves
¼ cup lemon juice
Black pepper

Roast garlic Preheat oven to 400°F.

Peel most of the skin off the heads of garlic, then trim the tops off the bulbs (¼ inch) to expose the tops of the cloves. Drizzle with oil. Wrap in aluminum foil and bake for 40 minutes, until soft and fragrant. Press cloves out of the skin and set aside. (Roasted garlic can be refrigerated for up to 2 weeks or frozen for up to 3 months.)

Wild nettle and sorrel soup Bring the water to a boil in a stockpot and add ¼ cup of salt. Using tongs, carefully lower nettles into the water, then stir and cook for 4 to 5 minutes, until tender. Drain nettles, then transfer them to a large bowl of ice water. Set aside for 1 to 2 minutes. Drain nettles again and set aside. At this point the sting won't be a concern, so the nettles will be easier to handle.

Heat oil in a medium saucepan over medium-high heat. Add leeks, celery and the chopped garlic and sauté for 3 to 5 minutes, until translucent. Add stock, potato, roasted garlic, thyme, hot sauce and the remaining 2 tablespoons salt. Simmer for 20 minutes, until potatoes have softened.

Add nettles, sorrel and lemon juice and stir to incorporate. Use an immersion blender, blend the soup until smooth and velvety. Season with salt and pepper.

Ladle into bowls and serve.

The Great Big Vegan Burger

SERVES 8 At SoBo, Lisa Ahier had always wanted to have a good vegan burger on offer but was unhappy with the pre-made frozen patties she'd tried. So she created her own. If you find the cumin and coriander in the spice mix too strong, she says, just leave them out—the burger will still be delicious.

Burger patties

1 cup dried black beans, rinsed

5 cups cold water (divided), plus extra if needed

2 tsp salt (divided)

½ cup quinoa

1 large portobello mushroom cap, finely chopped

¼ large red onion, finely chopped

3 to 4 cloves garlic, finely chopped

6 Tbsp olive oil (divided)

1 Tbsp balsamic vinegar

½ cup shelled pumpkin seeds

1 Tbsp flax seeds, ground

6 Tbsp water

½ carrot, grated

¼ cup finely chopped Italian parsley

Juice of 1 lemon

1 tsp ground cumin

1 tsp ground coriander

1 tsp chili powder

Assembly

8 hamburger buns, halved

20 to 30 baby spinach leaves (roughly 1 cup)

4 dill pickles, sliced lengthwise

½ cup ketchup

½ cup vegan mayonnaise (optional)

2 avocados, sliced

2 large beefsteak or heirloom tomatoes, sliced ½ inch thick

Burger patties Bring beans and 4 cups of cold water to a boil in a medium saucepan. Reduce heat to low, cover and simmer for 2½ to 3 hours, until tender. (If needed, add more water as beans simmer to prevent the mixture from running dry.) Add 1 teaspoon of salt, then drain beans and set aside to cool.

Preheat oven to 400°F.

Spread quinoa out on a baking sheet and toast for 5 minutes. Transfer to a medium saucepan, add the remaining 1 cup of water and bring to a boil. Reduce heat to low, cover and simmer for 11 minutes, until quinoa is light and fluffy. Drain quinoa, then spread it on the baking sheet to cool.

Spread mushroom, onion and garlic out on another baking sheet and drizzle ¼ cup oil and the vinegar overtop. Roast for 15 minutes, then set aside to cool.

Toast the pumpkin seeds on a baking sheet in the oven for 5 minutes. Remove from the oven and allow to cool.

Meanwhile, soak the ground flax seeds for 10 minutes in a small bowl filled with 6 Tbsp of water. The flax seeds are the burger patties' binding agent.

In a large bowl, combine beans, quinoa, the mushroom mixture, pumpkin seeds, the flax seed slurry, grated carrot, parsley, lemon juice, spices and the remaining teaspoon of salt and mix well. Add half of this mixture to a food processor and pulse for a few seconds until the beans start to break down. You are not looking for a

paste, you just want it to bind together so it can be shaped into patties. Remove and repeat the process with the other half of the mixture.

Using your hands, shape the mixture into 8 burger patties. (At this point, you can refrigerate or freeze the patties for future use. They can be kept for 3 to 4 days in the fridge, or up to 6 months frozen.)

Heat the remaining 2 tablespoons oil in a frying pan over medium-high heat. Add patties, working in batches if necessary to avoid overcrowding, and pan-sear for 3 minutes on one side. Flip over, reduce heat to medium and sear for another 3 to 4 minutes, until heated through.

Assembly Set the buns on your work surface or individual plates. Construct the burgers by adding the toppings.

Note: The burger patties require a degree of time to make, so it's worth freezing a batch of the patties or any extras for future use. Freeze separately on a baking sheet, then transfer them into a large zip-top bag and keep them flat in the freezer. Just adjust the toppings quantities accordingly.

The biggest challenge with vegan burger patties is that they tend to crumble due to the low level of fat in the recipe. These ones hold together pretty well, but if you're not a vegan, feel free to crack an egg into the mixture before pulsing in the processor.

SWEPT AWAY INN

Bouchra and Daniel Savard

Back when they were still living in Ontario, and before they fell in love with the West Coast, Daniel and Bouchra Savard took sailing lessons, and she cooked her favourite French-Moroccan dishes for the skipper. "You need to be cooking on a boat," he told them. And now they are.

The Swept Away Inn is a 100-foot tugboat called the MV *Songhee*, restored and converted (after a year and a half of hard work) into cosy accommodations, and docked at the Port Alberni waterfront. "We didn't want to operate a restaurant that was 24/7," Bouchra Savard says. "We wanted something unique."

A large part of the attraction for guests is her cooking. Savard emigrated from Morocco twenty-six years ago and still cooks the vibrant dishes of her homeland, even getting her sister to send her whole spices, which she roasts and grinds herself. "Spices here don't have the same potency. They don't even taste the same," she says.

"Just how the food is made, it's real whole food," Savard says. "Normally, we do two entrées—a salad, a soup—then we do the main, which is chicken, lamb, beef or fish. We serve that with the side dishes: couscous, lentils and eggplant. My husband does all the desserts. He's famous for his pomegranate cheesecake."

And although she is using Moroccan spices and following Moroccan recipes, she relies on organic ingredients from local farms. "I've learned so much from here, too," she says. "It is Moroccan cooking, but I'm adding my own twist to it."

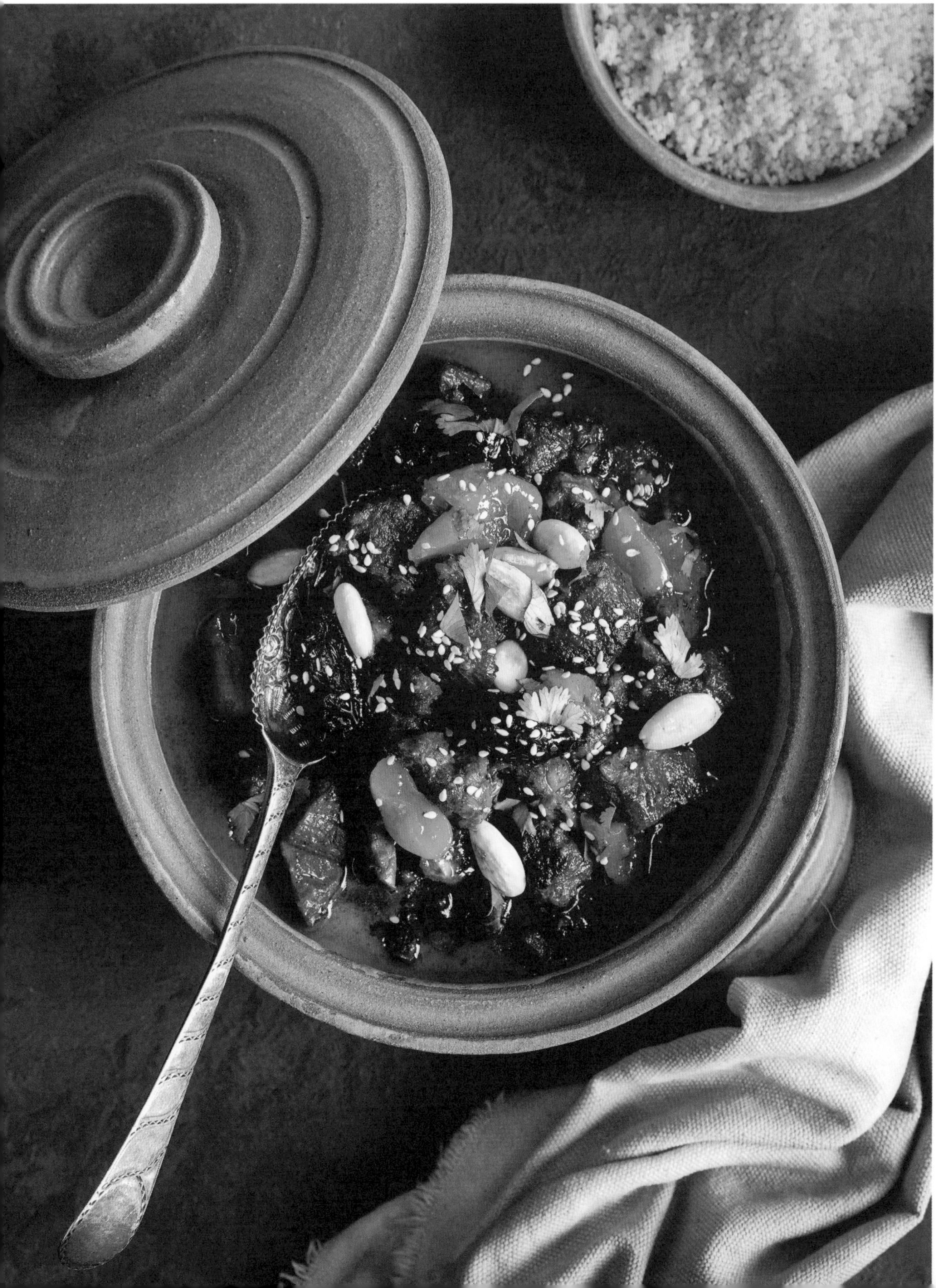

Lamb M'hamer with Prunes and Apricots, p. 160

Lamb M'hamer with Prunes and Apricots

SERVES 4 TO 6 This royal dish is served for celebrations in Bouchra Savard's native Morocco—and at the inn she and her husband have made from a tugboat in Port Alberni. She recommends making your own spice blend and grinding the spices fresh for the best flavour. However, if time doesn't allow, you can use a quality ras el hanout blend such as the one made by Clever Crow Farm in Black Creek.

Lamb tagine

4 lbs boneless leg of lamb, cut into 2-inch chunks

Salt and black pepper

Pinch of saffron

1¼ cups hot water (divided), plus extra if needed

⅓ cup olive oil

2 large red onions, thinly sliced

10 cloves garlic, crushed

6 Tbsp store-bought or homemade Ras el Hanout (see here)

2 bay leaves

¼ cup honey (divided)

2 Tbsp orange blossom water (divided)

1 Tbsp smen or ghee (see Note)

Handful of cilantro, finely chopped

Handful of Italian parsley, finely chopped

2 Tbsp butter

1 cinnamon stick

1⅓ cups dried apricots, sliced

1½ cups dried prunes

½ cup blanched almonds, toasted

2 Tbsp toasted sesame seeds

Chopped cilantro, for garnish

Couscous or rice, to serve

Ras el hanout

1½ Tbsp ground allspice

1 Tbsp ground turmeric

1 Tbsp ground cinnamon

1 Tbsp coriander seeds, crushed

1 tsp ground cardamom

1 tsp ground ginger

1 tsp crushed fennel seeds

1 tsp ground nutmeg

½ tsp ground clove

½ tsp cayenne pepper

Ras el hanout Mix all spices together in a small bowl and set aside. (Makes just over 6 tablespoons ras el hanout.)

Lamb tagine Preheat oven to 350°F.

Generously season lamb with salt and pepper and set aside at room temperature for 20 minutes.

In a small bowl, combine saffron and 1 cup hot water.

Heat oil in a Dutch oven or deep saucepan over medium-high heat. Add lamb and sear on all sides, using tongs to turn. Reduce heat, add onions and sauté for 5 to 10 minutes until softened. Add garlic, ras el hanout, bay leaves, 3 tablespoons honey, 1 tablespoon orange blossom water and smen (or ghee). Mix well, then add cilantro, parsley and saffron water and bring to a simmer. Cover and simmer for 15 to 20 minutes.

Place pan in the oven and cook for 1¼ to 1½ hours, until meat is caramelized and tender. (The juices released will mix with the spices to create a sauce without adding extra liquid.)

Meanwhile, in a separate saucepan, combine butter, the remaining ¼ cup water, the remaining 1 tablespoon of honey, 1 tablespoon orange blossom water and cinnamon stick and mix well. Add apricots and prunes and simmer for 20 minutes on low heat, until syrupy and the dried fruit have softened. If it becomes very dry, add a little more water.

Transfer lamb to a tagine pot or serving bowl. Top with prunes and apricots. Sprinkle almonds, toasted sesame seeds, and chopped cilantro on top and serve with couscous or rice.

Note: Smen, ghee, clarified butter—they are all variations on a theme. Clarified butter is simmered to remove the water, which creates a higher smoke point and makes it a terrific vehicle for high-temperature cooking. Ghee is traditional to South Asian cooking, and is cooked over low heat until the milk solids become lightly brown, nutty and caramelized. Smen is fermented butter from Morocco, made from sheep, cow or goat's milk, clarified, salt (and sometimes herbs) added, then aged until it becomes complex and a little funky. It is hard to find in North America; clarified butter makes a good substitute.

Pomegranate Cheesecake

SERVES 12 TO 16 For many guests at Swept Away Inn, Daniel Savard's cheesecake is one of the reasons they come back year after year. He recommends chilling it for at least 4 hours or preferably overnight before serving.

Crust

½ cup (1 stick) butter, room temperature

¼ cup packed brown sugar

1 egg

1½ cups flour

Filling

4 (250-g) packages cream cheese, softened

1¼ cups sugar

¼ cup flour

3 eggs

1 Tbsp vanilla extract

½ cup sour cream

Grated zest of 1 lemon

1 cup pomegranate seeds

Topping

1½ cups sour cream

¼ cup sugar

1 tsp vanilla extract

Pomegranate glaze

2 cups pomegranate juice

¼ cup packed brown sugar

1½ Tbsp cornstarch

Assembly

1 cup pomegranate seeds

Crust Preheat oven to 350°F.

In a mixing bowl, beat butter on medium-high speed for 30 seconds. Add brown sugar and beat until combined. Add egg and mix well. Add flour and mix until a dough forms. Divide dough in half, then cover one portion with plastic wrap and set aside.

Remove sides from a large (10- or 11-inch) springform pan and set aside. Spread the portion of dough so it covers the entire bottom of the ungreased pan. Place on a baking sheet and bake for 10 minutes, then set aside to cool. This creates a firm, cookie-like base.

Attach sides of the pan. Divide remaining dough into four equal pieces and roll them in your hands into 4 equal ropes, each 6 or 7 inches long. Press dough around the base and partway up the sides of the pan, connecting them together by using your thumbs to push the dough into place.

Filling Reduce oven temperature to 325°F.

In an extra-large bowl, combine cream cheese and sugar and beat until fluffy. Add flour and mix on low speed until smooth. Add eggs and vanilla and beat again on low speed, until just combined. Stir in sour cream and lemon zest.

Using a spatula, gently fold in pomegranate seeds. (Do not use a mixer—it will crush the seeds.)

Pour filling into pan. Place on a baking sheet and bake for 1 hour, until edges are puffed and centre is solid but jiggles slightly when gently shaken. Remove from oven. (It doesn't matter if the cheesecake cracks on top since it will have a sour cream topping.)

Topping In a bowl, combine sour cream, sugar and vanilla and mix well. Gently spread topping over cheesecake. Return to oven and bake for 10 minutes. Transfer to a wire rack and set aside to cool for 15 minutes.

Run an offset spatula around the cheesecake to loosen crust from sides of pan and cool for another 30 minutes. Remove the sides. Cool completely, then cover loosely and chill for at least 4 hours or overnight.

Pomegranate glaze Bring pomegranate juice to a boil in a medium saucepan. Reduce heat to medium and simmer, uncovered, for 12 to 15 minutes, until reduced to 1 cup.

In a separate bowl, stir together brown sugar and cornstarch. Add to the pan and stir constantly for 2 minutes, until thickened and bubbly. Cook and stir for another 2 minutes. Transfer to a medium bowl, then cover with plastic wrap right on the surface to prevent a film from forming. Let cool to room temperature then store, covered, in the fridge until needed.

Assembly Remove cheesecake and pomegranate glaze from fridge 15 minutes before serving. Spoon most of the glaze overtop, then top with pomegranate seeds, concentrating them in the centre. To serve, slice cheesecake and spoon remaining sauce over each slice.

TIDAL CAFÉ

Kurt and Blythe Reimer

After careers as military pilots—she was Canada's first female CH-124 Sea King ship-borne helicopter pilot and he flew the Lockheed C-130 Hercules aircraft—Blythe and Kurt Reimer loved their new community of Comox. There was just one thing missing: a really great breakfast place. So they opened their own.

"That was a no-brainer for us," Blythe says. "There wasn't a true breakfast place in Comox. And we love going to those classy yet cosy spots, like Blue Fox Cafe in Victoria or Café Medina in Vancouver." And besides, Kurt adds, "If we could have every evening free and a couple of days a week away from it, it wouldn't cut into our Island lifestyle."

They opened the bright and cheery Tidal Café in late 2019. Although they serve all the traditional breakfast classics, their signature dishes are the inventive bowls, like the Ranchero Bowl (house-made black bean patties and locally made tostadas) or Mo-Jo bowl (eggs and mushrooms over potato rösti, page 164). The Bennys are built on soft buttermilk biscuits rather than English muffins. And the buttermilk pancakes with berry compote and vanilla cream (page 163) follow the recipe the Reimers used to feed their three boys when they were growing up.

"We're proud of the fact that we use local free-range eggs, local pork and locally roasted coffee" Kurt says. "We can pick up our eggs right from the farmer and see all the chickens running around. It costs more, but we feel like we're giving back to the community."

Blythe adds, "People feel good when they come to our restaurant and know that they're not just supporting us, but also our providers."

Buttermilk Pancakes with Berry Compote and Vanilla Cream

SERVES 4 When Blythe and Kurt Reimer were raising their three sons, these pancakes were a staple in their home—and were so popular, they'd even gift the base to their friends at Christmas time. Now they've elevated them with a berry compote and vanilla cream.

Berry compote

1 cup frozen blueberries or berries of your choice

¼ cup sugar

1 Tbsp chopped basil, mint, rosemary or thyme (optional)

Vanilla cream

1¼ cups milk

2 Tbsp sugar

1 Tbsp cornstarch

1 tsp vanilla extract

2 egg yolks

Buttermilk pancakes

2 cups unbleached flour

2 Tbsp sugar

1 tsp baking powder

1 tsp baking soda

1 tsp salt

2 cups buttermilk

⅓ cup (⅔ stick) butter, melted

1 tsp vanilla extract

2 eggs

2 egg whites, room temperature

1 to 2 tsp canola oil

Maple syrup, to serve

Berry compote Combine berries and sugar in a small saucepan and simmer over medium heat, uncovered, for 15 minutes, until slightly thickened. Remove from heat, then stir in herb of choice (if using). (Compote can be stored in an airtight container in the fridge for up to 10 days.)

Vanilla cream Combine all ingredients in a small saucepan and whisk well over medium heat, until cream starts to boil and thickens enough to coat the back of a spoon.

Transfer to a bowl and set aside to cool slightly. (It can be stored in an airtight container in the fridge for up to 5 days.)

Buttermilk pancakes In a large bowl, combine flour, sugar, baking powder, baking soda and salt.

In a separate bowl, beat together buttermilk, butter, vanilla and whole eggs.

In a third bowl, beat egg whites until stiff peaks form.

Heat oil on a griddle or in a frying pan over medium-high heat. (To test the heat, flick water across the surface—if it beads up and sizzles, it's ready!) Having the pan hot and ready to go before you finish mixing the batter will help preserve the leavening effects that make the pancakes so fluffy.

Pour wet mixture into dry mixture and use a wooden spoon or fork to blend until just mixed. Fold in egg whites. Do not overmix or the egg whites will flatten!

Pour ½ cup batter into the pan and cook for 1 minute, until golden and bubbles begin to form on the surface. Turn over and cook for another 1 to 2 minutes. Transfer to a plate and repeat with remaining pancakes.

Serve hot, topped with berry compote and drizzled with vanilla cream and maple syrup.

Mo-Jo Bowl

SERVES 4 Inspired by the Reimers' son Joel and his girlfriend, Morgan, this is one of the most popular bowls at Tidal Café. It can easily be made vegan by substituting a tofu scramble for the eggs and topping it with vegan hollandaise. Or delight the meat lovers around the breakfast table by adding bacon or sausage.

Potato rösti

Cooking spray

4 to 6 Kennebec or yellow potatoes, unpeeled

1¼ lbs yam, peeled and shredded

1 Tbsp vegetable oil

1 small yellow onion, finely chopped (½ cup)

2 cloves garlic, finely chopped

2 tsp salt

½ tsp white pepper

Hollandaise sauce

3 egg yolks

1 Tbsp lemon juice

Dash of Tabasco sauce, or to taste

½ cup (1 stick) butter, cut into chunks

Salt and black pepper, to taste

Mo-Jo bowl

8 free-range eggs

Salt and black pepper, to taste

2 Tbsp olive oil or vegetable oil

1 to 2 cups white or cremini mushrooms, sliced

1 small red onion, chopped

1 large red bell pepper, seeded, deveined and chopped

1 large green bell pepper, seeded, deveined and chopped

8 Potato Rösti (see here)

2 Tbsp butter

Hollandaise Sauce (see here)

Microgreens or finely chopped green onions

Buttered toast, to serve

Potato rösti Preheat oven to 350°F. Spray a 12-cup muffin pan with cooking spray.

Place potatoes in a stockpot, cover with water and bring to a rolling boil. Boil for 5 minutes, then drain and set aside to cool.

Peel potatoes, then shred using a food processor or a box grater. Transfer shredded potato to a bowl and add shredded yam.

Heat oil in a small frying pan over medium-high heat. Add onion and garlic and sauté for 3 to 5 minutes, until softened and golden brown. Add to the potato mixture, then season with salt and white pepper. Gently mix to evenly incorporate, taking care not to smoosh the potatoes and ruin their texture.

Spoon heaping ¼-cup portions in the prepared muffin pan, then lightly press down. Bake for 40 minutes, turning pan after 20 minutes for even cooking. Makes 12 rösti. (The rösti can be stored in an airtight container in the fridge for up to 4 days or frozen for up to 3 months. When ready to serve, reheat on the grill from frozen until crisp on the outside and soft on the inside.)

Hollandaise sauce In a blender, combine egg yolks, lemon juice and Tabasco sauce.

Place butter in a microwavable bowl. Heat in the microwave for 20 to 30 seconds, or longer if needed, until completely melted and hot.

With the blender set on high speed, pour in butter in a thin stream. The sauce should thicken almost immediately. Season to taste. Keep warm until serving by setting blender pitcher in a pan of hot water.

Mo-Jo bowl Whisk together eggs, salt and pepper in a medium bowl. Heat oil in a large non-stick frying pan over medium-high heat. Add mushrooms, onion and peppers and sauté for 3 to 4 minutes until tender-crisp.

Place 2 potato rösti in each of 4 large bowls. Alternatively, arrange the röstis on plates to create a sort of benny. Divide vegetables evenly on top.

Melt butter in another non-stick frying pan over medium-high heat. Add eggs and scramble to desired doneness. Place on top of veggies, then ladle hollandaise sauce overtop. Garnish with microgreens (or green onions) and serve with buttered toast.

TOPTABLE VICTORIA

Kristian Eligh

Island foodies cheered when word got out that Toptable Group—the company behind legendary Vancouver restaurants like Blue Water Cafe, CinCin Ristorante + Bar, Elisa Steakhouse and Thierry Chocolates—was opening a restaurant in Victoria. The news that Victoria's own Kristian Eligh would be executive chef just made it all the sweeter.

Eligh, who began his career at the Brentwood Bay Resort (page 42), is best known from his years as the culinary director for Hawksworth Restaurant Group, helping lead the flagship Hawksworth Restaurant to be named the *Maclean's* Restaurant of the Year, among other accolades. But he has also staged in Michelin-starred kitchens including the French Laundry and Jean-Georges and worked as culinary development chef for Browns Restaurant Group.

"I fell in love with Vancouver, but I have a young family with two little girls and always wanted to make the move back," he says. "When I started discussions with Toptable, it was a no-brainer. The opportunity was something that really grabbed me."

What also grabbed him was the location: a stylish new building at Pandora and Douglas, in the up-and-coming financial district right across from City Hall. "The space we're creating is beautiful, inviting and bright. I don't think there is a room like it in Victoria," he says. "Our ambition is to provide a hospitality experience that speaks to the community with a sense of approachability."

The concept features coastal cuisine, sushi and a raw bar comprising locally and globally sourced seafood and produce. "I've started to forge relationships with local farmers," says Eligh, who lives in Saanich, surrounded by farms. "The romantic notion of me picking up groceries on my way to the restaurant by way of these farmers is not out of reach."

Broccoli Tartare with Fig, Almond and Mimolette Cheese

SERVES 4 At Victoria's new Toptable restaurant, chef Kristian Eligh is celebrating the great vegetables that grow on Vancouver Island. For this recipe he uses mimolette, a bright orange gouda-like cheese from Normandy. If you can't find it, use a firm aged cheddar instead.

Pickled shallots

⅓ cup red wine vinegar

2 Tbsp water

2 Tbsp sugar

2 large shallots, finely chopped

Broccoli tartare

¼ cup whole almonds

2 tsp salt, plus extra for sprinkling

3 to 4 heads broccoli, cut into ½-inch pieces (4 cups)

1¼ cups finely grated mimolette cheese (divided)

¼ cup diced dried Mission figs

¼ cup seasoned bread crumbs

6 Tbsp good-quality olive oil

3 Tbsp drained Pickled Shallots (see here)

2 Tbsp finely chopped Italian parsley

2 Tbsp lemon juice (preferably Meyer)

1 Tbsp sherry vinegar

1 tsp black pepper

1 tsp crushed red pepper

Pickled shallots Place vinegar, sugar and water in a small saucepan and bring to just under a boil on medium-high heat to dissolve the sugar. Place shallots in a non-reactive container or bowl. Pour warm pickling liquid overtop and set aside for at least an hour. (This can also be done in advance and stored in your fridge.)

Broccoli tartare Preheat oven to 350°F. Line a baking sheet with parchment paper.

Place almonds on the prepared baking sheet and roast for 8 to 10 minutes until lightly toasted. Lightly season with salt, then set aside to cool. Finely chop into ¼-inch pieces.

Combine all ingredients in a mixing bowl, reserving ¼ cup of mimolette cheese for later, and mix well.

Using a 6-inch ring mould, set portions onto 4 plates. (Alternatively, pile neatly in the centre of each plate.) Scatter the remaining ¼ cup mimolette cheese overtop and serve immediately.

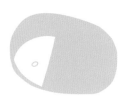

Dungeness Crab Dip with Toasted Sourdough

SERVES 4 TO 6 Dungeness crab is one of chef Kristian Eligh's favourite Island ingredients, and crab dip is one of his favourite ways to serve it. He's created a lighter, brighter, altogether more sophisticated variation that could take pride of place on any table. While sourdough is suggested here, this starter would also be great with toasted baguette rounds, or any of your favourite breads or crackers.

2 (1½-lb) whole Dungeness crabs or 14 oz fresh crabmeat, well-drained and picked of shells or cartilage

¼ cup (½ stick) butter

2 leeks, white and light green parts only, finely chopped

2 to 3 cloves garlic, finely chopped

2 tsp Old Bay seasoning

½ cup cream cheese

½ cup sour cream

8 cups spinach leaves

1 tsp Tabasco sauce

Grated zest of 1 lemon

1 Tbsp lemon juice

½ cup grated mozzarella

2 Tbsp finely grated Parmesan

1½ Tbsp finely chopped Italian parsley

1 tsp salt

Sliced sourdough, to serve

1 tsp olive oil, for drizzling

2 tsp chopped chives, for garnish

Lemon wedges, to serve

If you're starting with fresh whole crabs, bring a large saucepan of water to a boil. Add whole crabs and cook for 9½ minutes. Transfer crabs to a large bowl of ice water to cool down.

Remove the whole main shell (the carapace) from each crab in one piece so they can be used to serve the dip. Using a butter knife, scrape membranes from the inner walls of the shells. Rinse shells under hot water to remove all innards, then continue to clean and scrape the inside of the shell until clean.

Bring a large saucepan of water to a boil. Add the shells and boil for 5 minutes to sterilize. Reserve until needed.

Extract meat from the crabs. You should be left with 2 cups of crabmeat. Reserve.

Melt butter in a small saucepan over medium heat. Add leeks and garlic and sauté for 10 minutes. Be sure to stir often to avoid any colour on the leeks or garlic. Add Old Bay and cook for another 2 minutes.

Remove pan from heat, then add cream cheese and sour cream and stir until well mixed and cream cheese has melted. Transfer to a large bowl, then refrigerate until cool.

Bring a large saucepan of salted water to a boil. Add spinach and blanch for 30 seconds. Drain, then transfer to a bowl of ice water. Drain again, then squeeze spinach into a ball, extracting excess water. Finely chop spinach.

Take the leek and cream cheese mixture out of the fridge. Add spinach, Tabasco and lemon zest and juice. Stir in mozzarella, Parmesan, parsley and salt and mix well. Gently fold in crabmeat and evenly disburse while taking care not to break up large chunks of crab. (The dip can be stored in an airtight container in the fridge for up to 3 days.)

Preheat oven to 375°F.

Divide crab dip between the cleaned shells or transfer to a casserole dish and spread out evenly. Bake for 12 to 15 minutes.

Place sourdough on a baking sheet and lightly toast for 3 minutes.

Remove crab dip from oven and drizzle with oil. Sprinkle with chives, then serve immediately with toasted sourdough and lemon wedges.

TOQUE CATERING

Nicholas Waters

Given that he began his career cooking at prestigious properties like the Aerie, Wickaninnish Inn and Lumière, Nicholas Waters certainly had no intention of becoming a caterer in Victoria. But here he is. "At the beginning, I did it for a lifestyle change, because I have a family," he says. "But catering is a different monster, and I just fell for it. We're cooking nine separate and completely different dinners on a Saturday night. It's not a set menu. It's quite intense at the level we're trying to achieve. Either you have it or you don't."

Toque Catering handles all aspects of planning for everything from gourmet boxed lunches to corporate events, weddings and gala fundraisers. Menus are seasonally inspired, with almost endless options—they have seventy-two pages of menus and make 5,000 different types of canapés alone. They also work closely with some fifty farmers and foragers.

"We do everything. We do small intimate anniversary dinners for couples in their homes to corporate events serving five hundred people," he says. "We're known for our diversity and our canapés, our small bites."

It helps that he has a rock-star team of talented young chefs working with him, including Richard Teves, David Ediger, Janusz Urban, Clark Palfenier and Cathryn Kissinger. "We have the talent," Waters says. "Last year we were running full-time with thirteen executive chefs. We just sit at a round table and talk about food."

Beet and Lemon Goat Cheese Salad with Compressed Apples and Basil Vinaigrette, p. 172

Beet and Lemon Goat Cheese Salad with Compressed Apples and Basil Vinaigrette

SERVES 4 | Beets are chef Nicholas Waters's favourite vegetable, and they feature heavily on his menus at Toque Catering. Here, he offers them in a dramatic presentation, rolled with goat cheese and served with compressed apples and an herbaceous vinaigrette.

Beets

5 small red beets
5 small yellow beets
2 Tbsp apple cider vinegar (divided)
2 pods star anise (divided)
1 cinnamon stick, broken in half (divided)
3 Tbsp olive oil
2 Tbsp sherry vinegar
2 Tbsp chopped herbs, such as parsley, chives, basil and/or tarragon
Salt, to taste

Lemon goat cheese

½ cup fresh, creamy goat cheese
½ cup cream cheese
2 Tbsp chopped basil
1 tsp ground fennel seeds
1 tsp salt
1 tsp black pepper
Grated zest of 2 lemons

Beets Put red beets in a saucepan and add 1 tablespoon vinegar, 1 pod star anise and half a cinnamon stick. Repeat in a separate saucepan with the yellow beets. Cover beets with water and cook for 20 to 30 minutes on a gentle boil, until they can be pierced easily with a paring knife. Drain beets, then cool them under cold running water. Peel beets, keeping the colours separate.

Using a mandoline, carefully slice the beets of one colour very thin and set aside in a medium bowl. Cut the other beets into 1-inch cubes, or any attractive shape you like, and place in a separate bowl.

In a small bowl, whisk together the oil, vinegar, chopped herbs and salt, then divide the vinegar mixture between the two bowls of beets. Stir gently, then allow to marinate for 1 hour at room temperature.

Lemon goat cheese Combine all ingredients using a stand mixer fitted with a paddle attachment and mix for 5 minutes, until softened and well-combined. Transfer mixture to a piping bag.

Assembly Lay a 2-foot-long piece of plastic wrap on your work surface, the long side toward you. Starting 6 inches in from one end, lay out a row of sliced beets, overlapping each one, to a 12-inch length. Lay a second row of sliced beets beside it, just slightly overlapping the first row, so the two rows together create a 3- to 4-inch-wide sheet of beets that can be wrapped around the goat cheese. Pipe goat cheese along the entire length of the first row of beets. Using the plastic wrap as you would a sushi mat, roll the beets over the cheese and into a log, keeping air bubbles out, making sure it is firm and tight. Twist both ends of the plastic and tie. Reserve in fridge until needed.

If you have unused sliced beets, purée them in a blender until smooth, adding a touch of warm water if the purée is too thick (it should be spreadable). If you don't have enough sliced beets remaining, purée a small handful of the chopped beets instead. Or choose the beets of the colour you prefer.

Compressed apples Toss the apple slivers with olive oil, lemon zest and summer savory, then place in a vacuum sealer bag and seal airtight. This will remove the air from the bag, "compressing" the apples and immediately changing their texture. Store in the fridge until needed.

Note: Compressing apples in this way has two goals: first, to infuse them with the flavourings; and second, to make them softer and denser, giving them a "cooked" texture without the use of heat. If you don't have a vacuum sealer, you can approximate its effects by putting the ingredients in a resealable plastic bag, closing it most of the way, then inserting a straw and sucking as much air out as possible before sealing it fully. (Alternatively, you can seal all but a small corner of the bag, then dunk the rest of it in a bowl of water, allow the pressure of the water to press the air out of the bag and then finish sealing the bag.)

Basil vinaigrette Combine all ingredients in a blender and blend on low speed, then increase to high and mix until emulsified.

Assembly Remove plastic from the beet roll. Cut roll into 4 sections, each 3 inches long. Cut each section into 3 segments.

Spoon a tablespoon of beet purée onto a plate. Using the back of a spoon, spread it out as a long streak. Repeat with the 3 other plates. Arrange 3 beet pieces and 3 beet-and-goat-cheese slices on each plate.

Remove compressed apples from the vacuum bag. Arrange on top of beets. Sprinkle sea salt overtop, then drizzle basil dressing around beets.

Lightly toss arugula (or basil, sorrel or nasturtiums) with a few drops of olive oil and arrange attractively on the plates.

Compressed apples

2 Granny Smith apples, unpeeled, cored and cut into slivers

Grated zest of 1 lemon

1 tsp olive oil

2 Tbsp finely chopped summer savory

Basil vinaigrette

⅔ cup olive oil

3 Tbsp white balsamic vinegar

2 Tbsp chopped basil

1½ tsp Dijon mustard

1½ tsp maple syrup

½ tsp salt

¼ tsp black pepper

Grated zest and juice of ½ lemon

Assembly

Sea salt, to taste

Micro arugula leaves, basil leaves, sorrel leaves or nasturtiums, for garnish

High-quality olive oil

Butternut Squash Tortellini with Confit Tomatoes and Manchego Cheese

SERVES 6 The duck fat in chef Nicholas Waters's pasta dough is the secret ingredient that makes the tortellini so silky. Give yourself plenty of time to make this elegant crowd-pleaser, perfect for your next dinner party.

Pasta dough

1⅓ cups flour, plus extra for dusting
1 Tbsp duck fat
⅓ cup + 1½ tsp warm water, plus extra if needed
1 egg yolk
1 tsp olive oil
1 tsp salt

Butternut squash filling

3 cloves garlic, crushed
1 shallot, thinly sliced
3 or 4 sprigs thyme
1 Tbsp maple syrup
1 Tbsp salt
1 tsp black pepper
¼ tsp ground cumin
¼ tsp ground fennel seeds
¼ tsp ground coriander
¼ tsp Aleppo pepper
Grated zest of 3 lemons
1 (2-lb) butternut squash, peeled, seeded and cut into 1-inch cubes
1 cup (2 sticks) butter, cut into ½-inch cubes, plus extra for greasing

Pasta dough Lightly flour a baking sheet and set aside.

Mound the flour on a wood cutting board or clean work surface. Create a well in the centre, then use a fork to cut in the duck fat until mixed and crumbly.

Create another well in the centre of the mixture. Add the remaining ingredients to the well and use a fork or your fingers to mix with the crumbly flour. Knead dough for 5 minutes, until well combined and slightly springy to the touch. Add more water if the dough feels too stiff or dry.

Form into a ball, cover with plastic wrap, and rest for 30 minutes in the refrigerator.

Divide the dough into 2 equal pieces. Use a floured rolling pin to flatten each piece into a rectangle ½ inch thick. Cover any unused portions with a cloth or plastic wrap until needed. Roll the pieces of dough through a pasta machine, starting with the thickest setting and working to the thinnest, until each sheet is ⅛ inch thick and slightly translucent. (Alternatively, roll out the dough using a rolling pin.)

Lay pasta on the prepared baking sheet, then cover with damp dish towel and refrigerate until needed.

Butternut squash filling Preheat oven to 275°F and grease a baking dish.

In a large bowl, combine all ingredients except for squash and butter and mix well. Add squash and stir until coated, then transfer to a baking dish. Scatter butter cubes evenly over the squash, cover and bake for 3 hours, stirring every hour, until squash is soft and breaks apart with a fork. Remove the thyme stems and transfer the mixture to a food processor and purée until smooth. Allow to cool, then refrigerate in an airtight container until needed.

Confit tomatoes Combine all ingredients in a medium saucepan and cook for 5 to 10 minutes over low heat, until tomatoes start to blister and oil is slightly warm.

Drain confit tomatoes, reserving oil in a large bowl. Transfer tomatoes to a small bowl. Set both aside.

Butternut squash tortellini Place pasta dough on a lightly floured work surface. Using a 3-inch round cutter, cut pasta into rounds, spacing them as close to each other as possible. (Gather the scraps to re-roll and make more tortellini.) Using a spoon, place a tablespoon of filling in the centre of each round. Using a pastry brush, lightly brush beaten egg white on the pasta around the filling. Fold the dough over to form a half moon, using your fingers to press out air to avoid creating any air pockets. Draw the two corners together to form a bonnet shape. Repeat with remaining dough. Dust with flour, then cover and set aside.

Bring a large saucepan of water to a boil and add a generous pinch of salt. Working in batches to avoid overcrowding, gently lower tortellini into the water and cook for 4 to 6 minutes, until cooked through. Using a slotted spoon, transfer drained tortellini to the bowl of confit oil. Repeat with remaining tortellini and toss gently until coated.

Use slotted spoon to transfer tortellini to a serving dish. Spoon confit tomatoes overtop and finish with Manchego and basil leaves. Serve immediately.

Confit tomatoes

1 lb heirloom cherry tomatoes
2 cloves garlic, slivered
1 small shallot, thinly sliced
2 tsp thyme leaves
2 tsp chopped oregano
2 tsp chopped basil
2 tsp salt
1 tsp black pepper
1 tsp crushed red pepper
2 cups olive oil

Butternut squash tortellini

Pasta Dough (see here)
Flour, for dusting
Butternut Squash Filling (see here)
1 egg white, beaten
Salt
3½ oz Manchego cheese, shaved
Basil leaves, for garnish

TWIN CITY BREWING COMPANY

BJ Gillis

This craft brewery and kitchen is all about community spirit, in a town that's built on it.

"I grew up in Port Alberni, a small, sleepy mill town," says brewmaster and founder Aaron Colyn. "My plan was to go to medical school, but I got pulled into the science of fermenting. And I wanted to do something for my hometown that would create a social hub."

He launched a crowdfunding initiative to raise money to open his craft brewery and kitchen—the response was overwhelming, he says—and called it Twin City after a largely forgotten part of the community's past. Until the 1960s, it was actually two cities: the booming pulp-mill and port towns of Alberni and Port Alberni. Then in 1964, a tsunami, triggered by an earthquake in Alaska, surged up the inlet and destroyed much of both communities. It took teamwork to rebuild, and in 1967 they came together as one city. The same kind of teamwork that helped build Colyn's brewery.

He raised enough seed money to take over an old print shop and start making beer. "I wanted to make beer that was comparable to any on the Island," he says. And he hired chef BJ Gillis, who brings a global palate to pub favourites. Originally from Nova Scotia, Gillis had worked in Ontario and Alberta and at a fishing lodge in Bamfield when he and his wife decided to try Port Alberni for a year. "That was eleven years ago, and I don't know why the rest of the country doesn't live here," Gillis says. "We've just turned this place into home, and I love it."

His menu focuses on pizzas and smoked meats with high-end, often local ingredients, like the buffalo mozzarella and pepperoni from producers right in Port Alberni. The pizza dough goes through a three-day rise and the menu features international takes like banh mi pizza and tikka masala pizza. "I love that we draw inspiration from around the world and turn it into pizza," he says.

These days Port Alberni is seeing a rebirth due to businesses like Twin City Brewing. "It's going through a transformation," Colyn says. "There are a lot of young people who are doing cool things. There's been more change in the last five years than in the last twenty."

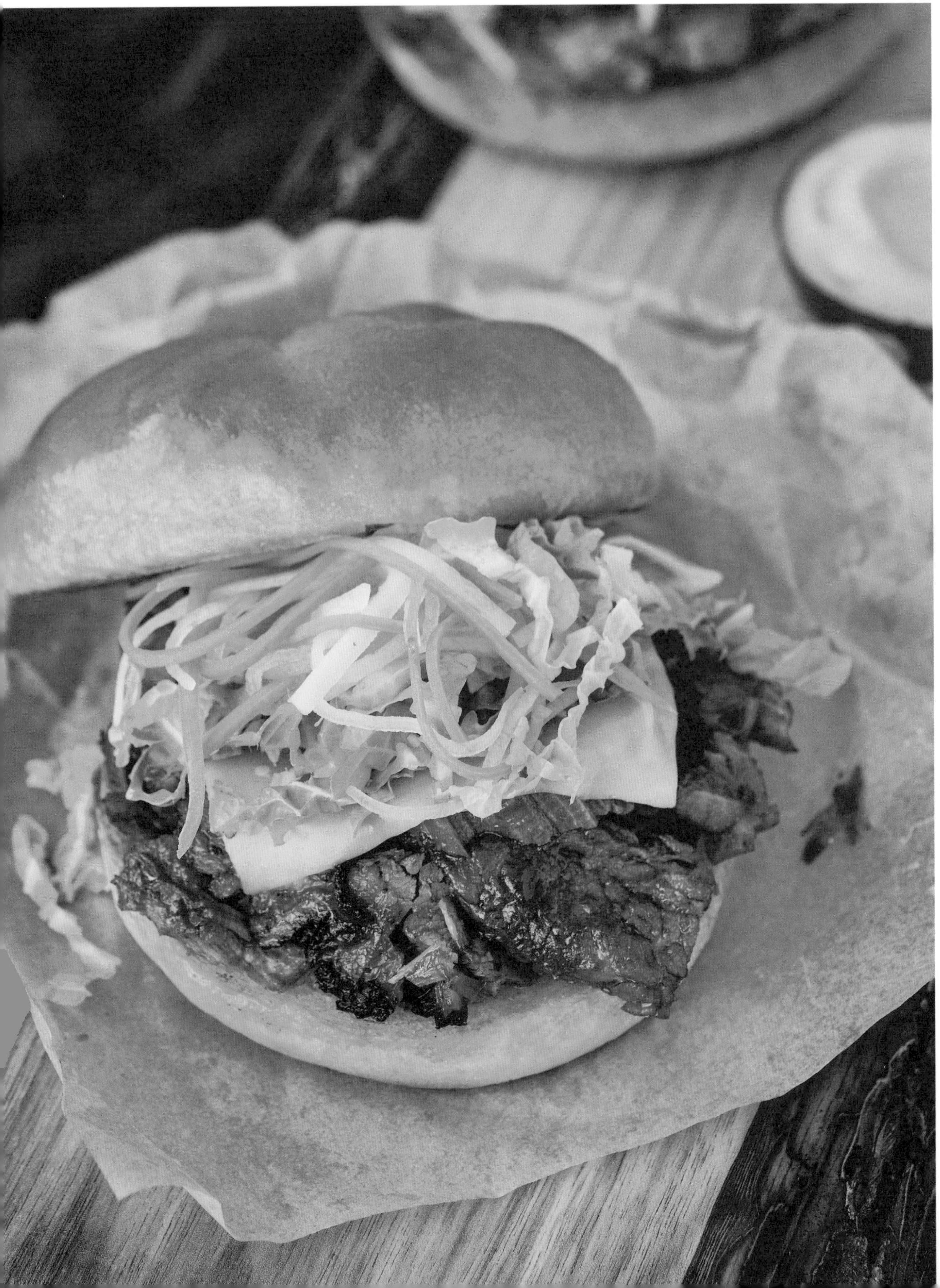

Bulgogi Brisket Sandwich, p. 178

Bulgogi Brisket Sandwich

SERVES 4 TO 6 At Port Alberni's Twin City Brewing, chef BJ Gillis makes this deconstructed bulgogi sandwich by combining slow-cooked beef brisket with tangy Asian flavours. Note that the brisket will need to cook for about four hours before it's fall-apart tender enough to be tucked into the brioche buns.

Brisket

1 pear, unpeeled and cored
3 cloves garlic, chopped
1 Tbsp chopped ginger
1 Tbsp crushed red pepper
1 Tbsp black pepper
2 cups beef stock or water
¼ cup tamari
2 Tbsp sesame oil
1 (3-lb) beef brisket

Carrot-daikon pickle

1 cup rice vinegar
½ cup water
2 Tbsp sugar
1 Tbsp salt
2 cups grated carrots
2 cups grated daikon radish

Gochujang aioli

1 small clove garlic, finely chopped
½ cup gochujang (Korean chili paste)
1 Tbsp mirin
1 Tbsp sesame oil
1 Tbsp tamari
1 Tbsp rice vinegar
1 Tbsp sugar
½ tsp finely chopped ginger
½ tsp fish sauce
1 egg
1 cup olive oil

Assembly

4 to 6 brioche hamburger buns, toasted
Grated or sliced mozzarella
1 to 1½ cups shredded napa cabbage
Carrot-Daikon Pickle (see here)
Gochujang Aioli (see here)

Brisket Preheat oven to 350°F.

Place all the ingredients except for the brisket in a food processor and purée until smooth. Set aside.

Heat a large frying pan over medium-high heat. Pat brisket with paper towel. Using a knife, score the fat, but not deep enough to cut into the meat. Place brisket in the pan and brown on all sides. Transfer brisket to a roasting pan, pour in the braising liquid and cover tightly with aluminum foil. Roast for 4 hours, until fork tender.

Carrot-daikon pickle Combine vinegar, water, sugar and salt in a large saucepan and bring to a boil over high heat.

Place carrot and daikon in a large Mason jar, pour in pickling brine, top with the lid and set aside for at least a few hours or overnight. (It can be stored in an airtight container in the fridge for 4 weeks.)

Gochujang aioli Place all ingredients, except for the egg and olive oil, into a food processor and purée until smooth. Add egg and process again until smooth. With the motor still running, gradually add oil and blend until emulsified. Transfer to a squeeze bottle and refrigerate until needed. It will thicken slightly in the fridge.

Assembly Once the brisket is fully cooked, remove from the pan. Slice or shred the meat. Mix with enough braising liquid to make it juicy, but not soggy.

Using tongs, set 4 to 6 ounces of meat onto the bottom buns. Top with mozzarella, cabbage and carrot-daikon pickle. Finish with gochujang aioli and place buns on top. Serve immediately.

Note: Unlike canning, which creates an environment where micro-organisms cannot grow, quick pickling is a short-term preservation process. Quick pickles must be refrigerated and consumed within a few weeks, and no more than 2 weeks for onions, garlic or mushrooms, which are especially susceptible to food-borne illnesses.

Coconut-Lime Cheesecake

SERVES 4 Put the lime in the coconut with this richly flavourful dessert from Twin City Brewing. Note that you will need four Mason jars or ramekins to make the individual portions.

¼ cup (½ stick) butter, melted

1 cup graham cracker crumbs

½ cup mascarpone, room temperature

½ cup cream cheese, room temperature

½ cup sugar (divided)

Grated zest and juice of 2 limes (divided)

¼ cup toasted coconut (divided)

1 tsp vanilla extract

1 cup whipping (33%) cream

Using your hands, mix butter and graham crumbs together in a bowl until well combined. Put 3 tablespoons of the crumble into 4 medium-sized ramekins or small Mason jars.

Using a stand mixer fitted with a paddle attachment, combine mascarpone and cream cheese. Add ¼ cup sugar, all the lime juice, half the lime zest, 2 tablespoons toasted coconut and the vanilla. Beat until smooth, then chill in the fridge until needed.

In a separate bowl, combine whipping cream and the remaining ¼ cup sugar and whip until stiff peaks form. Fold the whipped cream into the cheese mixture. Add ½ cup of the filling to each ramekin (or jar) and smooth the surface using the back of a spatula or a spoon.

In a small bowl, combine the remaining 2 tablespoons coconut and lime zest and mix well. Sprinkle some on top of each cheesecake and chill until ready to serve.

UNSWORTH RESTAURANT

Maartyn Hoogeveen

If anyone doubts the potential of the Cowichan Valley as a wine region, they need only look to Unsworth Vineyards. Tim and Colleen Turyk bought the property, with its early 1900s farmhouse, in 2009 and have since made a name for cool climate varieties like Pinot Gris and Pinot Noir. Their wines so impressed Barbara Banke, the chairman and proprietor of California-based Jackson Family Wines, that she and her daughter Julia Jackson bought the winery in 2019.

"They still want the Turyks to be involved with this for the long term," says Maartyn Hoogeveen, executive chef of the Unsworth Restaurant. (In fact, the Turyks' son Chris is the marketing director and sommelier.) "They're calling this the Napa of the North, and that is what they want to turn the Cowichan Valley into."

Hoogeveen himself is a relative newcomer, arriving here from his native New Zealand in 2015. "I love the Island. There's a lot of similarities between New Zealand and the Island, with the climate and the mountains," he says. And what he really loves is having the ingredients he gets to play with, such as the chanterelle, pine and lobster mushrooms that grow nearby. "We actually have local Benedictine monks—Brother Michael and Brother Francis—who forage the mushrooms for us," he adds. And it's not just the produce: "It's the seafood as well, the Salt Spring Island mussels and Vancouver Island's absolutely spectacular clams."

They go into his popular seafood chowder, one dish that will never come off the menu, and which pairs surprisingly well with the Prosecco-like sparkler Charme de L'Île. Though perhaps his favourite pairing is the Pinot Noir with braised lamb croquettes, cooked with cumin, fennel seeds and coriander. As Chris Turyk explains, "The Pinot brings out the complexity of the spices, which in turn make the red fruit notes of the wine sing higher."

As a winery restaurant, they serve mainly their own wines, of course, and that inspires Hoogeveen to pair his food to the wine. "It's the opposite of how it works in most kitchens," he says. "It's about tailoring the food to the wine here."

Island-Foraged Chanterelle Risotto

SERVES 4 | Local monks find wild mushrooms for Unsworth Restaurant, but you will likely have to forage for your own at the supermarket. If you can't find chanterelles, replace them with other flavourful varieties such as oysters or morels, although even plain white mushrooms will do. And if you are not vegetarian, you can always use chicken stock instead of mushroom, if you prefer.

Unsworth sommelier Chris Turyk suggests pairing the risotto with the Allegro white blend. "The 2019 Allegro is a white blend like no other. Don't be afraid of richness and creaminess in this preparation—Allegro cuts right through it and the woodsy notes of mushrooms and the complex flavours of the cheese are perfectly juxtaposed by the peach and yellow apple notes of the wine."

½ cup (1 stick) + 2 Tbsp butter (divided)

1 lb chanterelle mushrooms, cleaned

Salt and black pepper, to taste

3 cups mushroom stock

2 Tbsp olive oil

1 small onion, finely chopped

3 cloves garlic, crushed

1 cup arborio rice

½ cup Unsworth Vineyards 2018 Allegro white wine

½ cup grated Parmesan

¼ cup crumbled chèvre (preferably from Haltwhistle Cheese Company)

2 Tbsp chopped tarragon

¼ cup sliced almonds, toasted

Melt 2 tablespoons of butter in a large frying pan over medium heat. Add chanterelles and sauté for 4 to 5 minutes, until softened. Season with salt and pepper and set aside.

Bring stock to a boil in a small saucepan. Reduce heat to medium-low and leave at a simmer.

Heat oil in a medium saucepan over medium heat. Add onion and sauté for 1 minute. Add garlic and cook for another few seconds—do not let onion or garlic take on any colour. Add rice and cook for another 1 to 2 minutes, stirring, until rice is slightly translucent and well covered in oil.

Stir in the wine and cook until liquid has been reduced by three-quarters. Add a ladle of hot stock and cook, stirring frequently, until liquid has been almost completely absorbed. Continue this process until the rice is al dente and creamy and most, if not all, of the stock

has been used, about 25 minutes in total. Cube the remaining ½ cup (1 stick) butter. Remove pan from heat and quickly stir in butter, Parmesan and chèvre, until well combined. Add tarragon and half the chanterelles. Season with salt and pepper.

Divide risotto among 4 bowls, then top with the remaining chanterelles and toasted almonds.

Steamed Vancouver Island Clams

SERVES 4 Since arriving from New Zealand a few years ago, chef Maartyn Hoogeveen of Unsworth Vineyards has fallen in love with B.C. seafood, especially the clams. To make sure you don't get grit in the dish, he advises "purging" the clams by placing them in cold water for 5 to 10 minutes so they spit out any sand. (Most store-bought clams will have been purged already.)

As for the wine pairing, Unsworth sommelier Chris Turyk says, "This dish is crying for Vancouver Island Pinot Gris. Our 2019 Saison Vineyard Pinot Gris has both the breadth of flavour and enough texture to stand shoulder to shoulder with the acidity of the tomato and the fennel, which is sometimes tricky to pair. Although not full in body, our Pinot Gris has some weight to complement its vibrancy and the clams bring out the wine's slightly salty or saline notes."

3 Tbsp canola oil

1 lb tricolour cherry tomatoes

5 cloves garlic, crushed

1 shallot, finely chopped

1 bulb fennel, finely chopped, and fronds chopped and reserved

1 serrano pepper, seeded, deveined and finely chopped

2 lbs live clams, purged

1 cup Unsworth Vineyards 2019 Pinot Gris

1 cup (2 sticks) butter, cubed

¼ cup chopped Italian parsley

Salt and black pepper, to taste

Fresh focaccia, to serve

Heat oil in a large saucepan over high heat, until it just starts to smoke. Add tomatoes and pan-fry for 1 minute, until slightly blistered. Add garlic, shallot, chopped fennel bulb and serrano pepper and cook for another 4 to 5 minutes over high heat, until vegetables are soft and fragrant.

Add clams, Pinot Gris and butter. Cover, reduce heat to medium and cook for 3 to 5 minutes, until clams have opened up. Discard any unopened clams. Cook for another 3 to 4 minutes until the sauce has reduced down by a third.

Stir in parsley and half the fennel fronds, then season to taste. Transfer to serving bowls and scatter the remaining fennel fronds on top. Serve with fresh focaccia—and the remaining Pinot Gris.

WILD POPPY MARKET / OLD TOWN BAKERY

Kate Cram

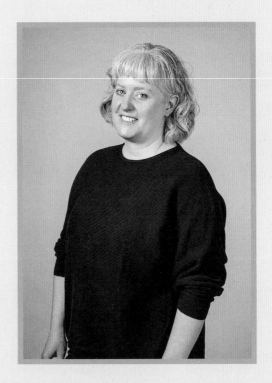

How the Vancouver Island food scene has changed in the last couple of decades "is just incredible," says Kate Cram, the chef-owner of Wild Poppy Market and Old Town Bakery. When she was in high school, she knew she'd have to leave if she wanted to be a serious chef and hightailed it to the Culinary Institute of America. "I turned eighteen and five days later moved by myself from Ladysmith to New York state," she says.

But she always knew she wanted to come back to the Island. For a while, she worked at a high-end luxury resort, but soon realized that it wasn't a good fit for the priorities in her life: "It wasn't me. And I have three children I'm passionate about." So in 2003 she opened a bakery where she was able to share many family recipes, especially the cinnamon buns that put her on the map. "My nineteen-year-old literally grew up in the bakery," she says. "I like to think of the bakery as a comfortable place for people."

A decade later she opened the bistro, serving mindfully sourced and prepared meals such as sandwiches, fish tacos, quiche and homemade soups. The pandemic of 2020 inspired her to change her business model, transforming the bistro into a market, where she carries grab-and-go meals and baked goods—including a big selection of gluten-free products—many of them made with ingredients sourced within the Cowichan Valley.

"My heart is on the Island," Cram says. "It's so abundant. We have the fresh seafood, the meat, the produce. We're really lucky to be here. There is nothing better than fresh salmon off the boat."

She adds: "The Island, but especially the Cowichan Valley, is on fire right now with so many farms, local producers and wineries. There's so much opportunity for chefs to do what they really enjoy right now. It's magical for me with the market, pulling all these ingredients together within this hub. It can't be anything but great."

Shrimp and Cod Cakes with Sweet Dijon Aioli

SERVES 4 | At Wild Poppy Market, chef-owner Kate Cram has developed a loyal following for the kinds of gluten-free treats (like this dish) that are impossible to find anywhere else. Upon learning that she herself was severely gluten intolerant, she studied holistic nutrition. As she says: "I wanted families like ourselves to have a safe place to eat."

Sweet Dijon aioli

2 cloves garlic

Sea salt

1 egg yolk

1 Tbsp lemon juice

½ tsp Dijon mustard

½ tsp grainy Dijon mustard

¼ cup olive oil

2 Tbsp vegetable oil

1 Tbsp honey

Black pepper

Shrimp and cod cakes

⅔ cup shelled and ground pumpkin seeds

½ cup cornmeal

1½ lbs fresh Pacific cod, finely chopped

1½ cups fresh baby shrimp

2 green onions, chopped

½ red bell pepper, seeded, deveined and finely chopped

⅓ cup corn kernels

¼ cup gluten-free bread crumbs

2 Tbsp gluten-free flour

1 Tbsp finely chopped dill

1 egg

¼ cup olive oil mayonnaise

3 to 4 dashes Tabasco sauce

1 tsp sea salt

¼ tsp black pepper

2 Tbsp olive oil

Fresh greens, to serve

Sweet Dijon aioli Using a chef's knife, finely chop garlic with a pinch of salt to make a paste. Set aside.

In a bowl, whisk together egg yolk, lemon juice and the mustards.

In a small bowl, combine oils, then add to the yolk mixture a few drops at a time, whisking constantly until emulsi-fied. Whisk in garlic paste and honey, and season with salt and pepper. If the aioli is too thick, whisk in 1 or 2 drops of water. Chill until needed.

Shrimp and cod cakes Preheat oven to 350°F.

Combine ground pumpkin seeds and cornmeal in a bowl. Set aside.

In a separate bowl, combine cod, shrimp, green onions, red pepper, corn, bread crumbs, flour and dill. Fold together until combined.

In a third bowl, combine egg, mayonnaise, Tabasco sauce, salt and pepper and mix well. Fold egg mixture into the cod mixture and mix until evenly combined.

Divide mixture into 8 balls, then flatten into patties 1 inch thick. Coat cakes in the cornmeal mixture and set them on a plate.

Heat oil in an ovenproof heavy-bottomed frying pan over medium heat. Add cakes to the pan and fry for 2 minutes, until golden brown. Flip and cook for another 2 minutes. Place pan in the oven and bake for 7 to 8 minutes, until the cakes are cooked through. Serve with fresh greens and sweet Dijon aioli.

Sliced Almond Cinnamon Buns with Cream Cheese Frosting

MAKES 9 BUNS At Ladysmith's Old Town Bakery, chef-owner Kate Cram makes nine different types of cinnamon buns—and these are one of her all-time favourites.

Dough

1⅓ cups milk

4 cups flour, plus extra for dusting

2½ tsp instant yeast

¼ cup sugar

¾ tsp salt

2 eggs, beaten

¼ cup (½ stick) butter, melted

Oil, for greasing

Cinnamon-sugar filling

1¼ cups golden yellow brown sugar

1½ tsp ground cinnamon

Cinnamon buns

Non-stick cooking spray, for greasing (optional)

Flour, for dusting

½ cup (1 stick) butter, room temperature

Dough (see here)

Cinnamon-Sugar Filling (see here)

½ cup sliced almonds

Cream cheese frosting

½ cup cream cheese (half a 250 g package)

3 Tbsp butter, room temperature

¾ cup icing sugar

½ tsp vanilla extract

Dough Warm milk in a small saucepan to a temperature of 110°F. This is warm enough to activate the yeast, but not hot enough to kill it or cause it to overproof.

Using a stand mixer fitted with a paddle attachment, combine flour, yeast, sugar and salt and mix until well combined.

In a separate bowl, combine eggs, warmed milk and butter and whisk together.

Add wet mixture to the dry mixture. Using a dough hook, mix dough on low speed for 90 seconds, until just combined. Increase speed to medium and mix for another 5 minutes. The dough will be sticky and may not completely clear the bottom of the bowl—this is to be expected.

Transfer dough to an oiled bowl, then cover with a dish towel. Set aside for 1 to 1½ hours, until dough has doubled in size.

Cinnamon-sugar filling In a small bowl, combine sugar and cinnamon and mix well. Set aside.

Cinnamon buns Prepare a 9-inch square pan with cooking spray or line it with parchment paper.

Place dough on a floured work surface. Roll dough into an 18- × 10-inch rectangle. Using a spatula, spread butter evenly across the surface of the dough. Sprinkle cinnamon-sugar on top. Scatter almonds evenly on top. Starting at one long side, roll up the dough into an 18-inch log.

Cut the log into 9 pieces, each 2 inches wide. Place cinnamon rolls face up into the prepared pan in 3 × 3 rows, evenly spaced. Cover with a dish towel and set aside for 30 minutes to rise.

Preheat oven to 350°F.

When the oven is ready, uncover the pan—the rolls will have risen and filled it—and place on the middle rack in the oven. Bake for 36 minutes in a convection oven (or 45 minutes in a regular one), until buns are lightly golden on top and the centre springs back when gently pressed. Set aside for 3 minutes to rest.

Carefully invert pan onto a baking sheet, being mindful that the sugar is very hot. Set aside for another 10 minutes to cool slightly.

Cream cheese frosting Using an electric mixer, combine all ingredients and mix until smooth and fluffy.

Ice buns and serve immediately.

WOODSHED PROVISIONS

Haidee Hart

Haidee Hart grew up on the west coast with "a deep appreciation of wild ingredients." That appreciation only grew when she moved to Salt Spring Island with her husband in 1995, and then ten years later became the chef at a celebrated local farm retreat. She stayed there for fifteen years, "steeped in the culture of food coming right in from the fields," until late 2019 when she and her family bought a little property close to the ocean.

While at the retreat, she had occasionally staged at places such as Chez Panisse and Quince in San Francisco and connected with food leaders in California, Italy and France. "That's my formal training—spending time in the most incredible fine-dining kitchens," Hart says. "I learned so much being mentored by the most incredible chefs."

The plan was to do more of the kind of travelling, teaching and learning she'd already started to do. Then a global pandemic hit, and Hart was grounded. One day she made some jars of her favourite soups and left them in her woodshed for her neighbours who were self-isolating, and Woodshed Provisions was born. Now she spends her days baking and making soups, salads and picnic fare from hyper-seasonal local ingredients, as well as working with a new food-delivery initiative called WAWWE (for "we are what we eat"). She's so busy she can't keep up with demand.

It's all self-serve, with customers leaving payment in a cash box carved out of a salvaged tree stump. "There's something about it that is very special," Hart says. "People are so appreciative of what we are doing and so honest. It is very humbling."

She still plans to get back to learning and teaching in the kitchen and hosting harvest dinners, but for now she's happy selling beautiful food from her woodshed. "It's just been a huge gift of this time," she says. "If you can share food that's thoughtfully procured, delicious and nourishing, while helping people feel cared for—I feel pretty good about that."

Cherry Tomato–Ricotta Galette, p. 190

Cherry Tomato–Ricotta Galette

SERVES 4 This is one of chef Haidee Hart's "absolute favourite" recipes. It makes enough pastry for two 9-inch galettes, and enough filling for one—you can double up on the filling ingredients and make two galettes or freeze half of the pastry to use later. Serve with a crisp salad and a glass of rosé.

Pastry

2½ cups unbleached flour, plus extra for dusting

2 tsp sugar

1 tsp salt

1 cup (2 sticks) cold butter, cut into cubes

4 to 6 Tbsp cold water

Galette

Pastry (see here)

1 cup ricotta

1 to 1½ lbs cherry tomatoes (preferably tricolour), halved

1 tsp salt

Small handful of chopped herbs, such as basil, thyme, tarragon and/or oregano

1 egg

Pastry Preheat oven to 375°F. Line a baking sheet with parchment paper.

Combine flour, sugar and salt in a food processor. Add butter and pulse until mixture has the consistency of cornmeal. Add 4 tablespoons cold water, processing just until the dough holds together. Add a bit more water, ½ tablespoon at a time, if needed.

Turn dough out onto a lightly floured work surface (a piece of floured parchment keeps the mess to a minimum) and divide the dough into 2 disks, ½ inch thick. Wrap the second disk of dough tightly in plastic wrap and freeze for later use.

Roll pastry out to an 11-inch circle, then trim any ragged edges. Place onto the prepared baking sheet. Chill in the fridge for 20 minutes.

Galette Spread ricotta evenly over galette pastry, to 2 inches away from the edge (you will fold this edge up onto the filling). Arrange tomatoes, cut-side down, over the ricotta. Tomatoes can be arranged in a single layer with a few added as another layer on top for great contrast in texture and colour. Tuck herbs in among the tomatoes. Sprinkle with salt.

Fold pastry edge up onto the tomatoes, which will leave some of the tomatoes and herbs showing. In a small bowl, combine egg and a teaspoon of water and mix well. Brush egg wash over folded pastry. Bake for 45 to 60 minutes, until pastry is golden brown and tomato juices are bubbling. Set aside to cool, then serve.

Apple Crisp

SERVES 4 TO 6 Salt Spring Island is famous for its bountiful apple harvest—a reported 400 varieties grow here, many of them heirloom species that have all but vanished elsewhere. They star in this simple and satisfying crisp from Haidee Hart, the chef-owner of Woodshed Provisions. She likes to vary the sizes of the slices to add texture to the crisp and advises that you can use a variety of apples, pears or a combination.

½ cup (1 stick) butter, room temperature, plus extra for greasing

5 to 6 apples, peeled, cored and sliced ½ inch thick (6 cups)

2 Tbsp + ¾ cup brown sugar (divided)

2 tsp ground cinnamon (divided)

½ to ¾ tsp ground cardamom (optional)

1½ cups oats

1 cup flour or gluten-free flour blend

1 tsp salt

Whipped cream or ice cream, to serve

Preheat oven to 350°F. Grease a 9-inch square or round baking dish.

In a large bowl, combine apples, 2 tablespoons brown sugar, 1 teaspoon cinnamon and cardamom (if using) and mix well. Transfer to the prepared baking dish.

In another large bowl, combine the ¾ cup brown sugar with the oats, flour, salt and the remaining 1 teaspoon cinnamon. Using your fingers, work butter into the dry ingredients until pea-sized pieces form.

Cover apples with the topping, pressing some of the topping into the fruit. Bake for 40 minutes, until golden brown, bubbling and very fragrant.

Serve with whipped cream (or ice cream).

ACKNOWLEDGEMENTS

Rounding up forty chefs and their recipes for a cookbook is never easy. Doing it during a global pandemic, well . . . let's just say producing this book has been a real labour of love, one we couldn't have completed without the help of many, many people.

It starts, of course, with the chefs, bakers, producers and restaurateurs in these pages.

Vancouver Island and the surrounding islands are blessed with incredible ingredients and even more so with talented people who transform those ingredients into delicious things to eat. That they all seem to be unusually kind, generous and thoughtful made this book a joy to work on. Thank you all for your time, your stories, your wonderful recipes and your patience in answering our many questions.

It has also been a real delight working with everyone at Figure 1. Thank you to Chris Labonté and Richard Nadeau for staying with the project despite the challenges the pandemic kept throwing our way. And thank you to all the editors who treated our words with so much care: managing editor Lara Smith, senior editor Michelle Meade, copy editor Pam Robertson and proofreader Merel Elsinga. You made our words sing and made sure we really knew our quick-pickled onions.

This book is a sumptuous visual feast thanks to a talented design and photography team. Thank you to Figure 1 creative director Naomi MacDonald for wrangling this complicated photo project with such grace, and for your overall vision of this book. Danika McDowell went beyond any reasonable call of duty to shoot our chefs in their natural habitat; meanwhile, Gabriel Cabrera beautifully translated their dishes long distance in the Vancouver studio with the help of food stylists Bri Beaudoin and Sophie MacKenzie. And we could not be more smitten with the illustrations by Ben Frey.

Too many cooks, they say, spoil the broth, but luckily that doesn't seem to apply to cookbook authors—or at least, not these ones. Dawn and Joanne first worked together at *Edible Vancouver Island* and then, over wine, hatched a plan for a cookbook celebrating the Island's great food scene. They feel very fortunate to have worked with each other on this project, and, as soon as it's allowed, are planning to meet for hugs and more wine.

On a personal note: Joanne would like to thank Lionel Wild for being the best quarantine companion possible and for his heroic work in sampling all the recipes tested. Dawn would like to thank her husband, Les, for his unwavering support, and her entire family for being willing subjects during the recipe testing phase. She would also like to thank Julie Ovenell for giving her confidence in the world of print media, and to Danika McDowell for joining her on the incredible *Edible* ride.

Vancouver Island is a magical place, and it has been a true honour to tell its culinary story. We can't wait until you taste what we've created here!

INDEX

ABOUT THE AUTHORS

Dawn Postnikoff

As co-founder of *Edible Vancouver Island*, Dawn Postnikoff shares her passion for coastal living and the local food and beverage culture with the *Edible* community. Having left the corporate world to become an entrepreneur several years ago, she now has multiple projects on the go, most of which focus on promoting culinary tourism throughout the region. Dawn is mom to five "mostly grown-up" children and loves spending time outdoors when she isn't playing in her kitchen or sipping wine with friends.

Joanne Sasvari

Joanne Sasvari grew up on Vancouver Island and in her heart, never left. She is the editor of the magazines *Vitis*, *The Alchemist* and *Westcoast Homes & Design* and writes about food, drink and travel for *Edible Vancouver Island*, Destination BC's Hello BC website, the *Vancouver Sun* and other Postmedia brands, and various other publications, including *Food & Wine* magazine. She is also the author of the IACP-shortlisted book *The Wickaninnish Cookbook, Vancouver Eats, Frommer's EasyGuide to Vancouver and Victoria* and *Paprika*. She lives in North Vancouver and is hungrily planning her next trip back to Vancouver Island.

The Series

Canada
Calgary Cooks
Calgary Eats
Edmonton Cooks
Montreal Cooks
Island Eats
Ottawa Cooks
Toronto Cooks
Toronto Eats
Vancouver Eats
Winnipeg Cooks

United States
East Bay Cooks
Houston Cooks
Miami Cooks
Phoenix Cooks
Portland Cooks
Seattle Cooks

Figure .1